THE PARKOUR
& FREERUNNING
HANDBOOK

DAN EDWARDES

About the author

Dan Edwardes is co-founder of Parkour Generations, the world's largest freerunning association. Edwardes completed his undergraduate and postgraduate degrees at Cambridge University and then spent several years in Japan and Southeast Asia continuing his lifelong practice of various fighting arts and movement disciplines. He teaches freerunning internationally and has produced a considerable body of literature on parkour that has been translated into several languages and published across various media. Edwardes lives in London. Visit Parkour Generations at www.ParkourGenerations.com.

THE PARKOUR & FREERUNNING HANDBOOK

DAN EDWARDES

An Imprint of HarperCollins*Publishers*

HarperCollins books may be purchased for educational, business,
or sales promotional use. For information, please write: Special
Markets Department, HarperCollins Publishers, 10 East 53rd Street,
New York, NY 10022.

FIRST EDITION

Designed by Jon Wainwright
Illustrations by Stefanie Coltra
(illustration on p. 22 by Richard Burgess)

Picture credits:
Andy Day: pp. 9, 12, 15, 26, 28, 31, 38, 41, 44, 47, 48, 51, 52, 57, 60,
63, 66, 69, 71, 74, 76, 80, 82, 140, 142; Paul Holmes: p. 34;
Corbis: pp. 25, 37; Getty Images: cover (ULTRA.F, ColorBlind
Images, and Chris McGrath), p. 84; iStockphoto: p.16
Printed on acid-free paper

Library of Congress Cataloging-in-Publication Data
is available upon request.

ISBN-10: 0-06-178367-6

ISBN-13: 978-0-06-178367-8

Conceived and produced by
Elwin Street Limited
144 Liverpool Road
London N1 1LA
www.elwinstreet.com

Printed in China

Author Acknowledgments

I would like to present my deepest thanks and respect to those
who have become my friends, brothers, and teachers in this art
of movement, in particular Forrest, Stephane, Tracey, Johann,
Kazuma, and Thomas—and also to everyone at Parkour
Generations and Majestic Force for being an ongoing
inspiration. Perhaps most importantly of all, I would like to
acknowledge and thank those nine men from France who
began this revolutionary—and evolutionary—movement,
first called *L'art du déplacement*. The Yamakasi spirit infuses
the discipline around the world to this very day.

Foreword

I n the fall of 2004, as I was branching out from the martial arts into acrobatics and stuntwork, I began searching the Internet for inspiration and guidance. Having picked up a few simple flips and techniques on my own, I was looking for ways to take my movement to the next level.

Through videos, forums, and a good bit of luck, I found my way into the British freerunning community, and instantly fell in love. The power, grace, and freedom of movement I was witnessing was exactly what I had been looking for—men and women unfettered by the environment around them, limited only by their willingness to work and their own imaginations.

And that's where the story of the American scene began—practitioners dotted across the States, isolated, uncertain, and almost entirely dependent on the Internet. In those days, our best sources of information were our friends in England, and runners, gymnasts, soldiers, and martial artists who never quite understood what it was we were asking them to help us with.

We were making our way through unknown territory, and it showed. Minor injuries plagued everyone. Innovation was slow and creativity faltered. Misconceptions were rife—we had examples of the final product before us, we could see the movements, we knew the possibilities—but we had no idea what steps to take to get there ourselves.

Life in the U.S. is different now. The revolution of movement has very much reached our shores, and those of us who survived those first rough years are finally in a position to guide others along the right path. The American scenes are thriving, and fewer and fewer newcomers are struggling the way that we did. There is a growing body of knowledge among the experienced practitioners, which is constantly becoming more available to the community as a whole. And this book is part of that: Whatever you are looking for in this world of movement, you hold in your hands exactly the right tool. You just need to get out there and use it.

Duncan Germain (a.k.a. "TK17")

Contents

Introduction:
a brief history of parkour

Since the late 1990s, a phenomenal new activity has exploded into the mainstream consciousness, infusing everything it touches with dynamism, vibrancy, and raw energy. That activity is known as "freerunning" or "parkour."

HUMBLE ORIGINS

Still young, this activity has spread from early life on French city streets to school sports education courses in the UK to live stage shows and cinema screens in Hollywood.

In one sense, parkour has existed for as long as man has moved either out of necessity, for enjoyment, or for practice. It exists as the basis of all human movement, from the play of children to the lifestyles of tribal cultures and from the discipline of the traditional martial arts to the methodology of modern athletics. Yet rarely, if ever, before has this essence of movement been applied in such a coherent and meaningful fashion.

The art of displacement infuses our movement with newfound life and vibrancy and a purpose that resonates deep within us. It is an expression of the natural beauty, power, grace, and efficiency of the human body, as well as a manifestation of the limitless potential of the human spirit.

" This phenomenon is known as freerunning or parkour. However, its roots go back to a time when it was originally called *L'art du déplacement* (the art of displacement). "

THE FRENCH CONNECTION

This powerful new philosophy was first revealed to the world by a group of nine young men from the suburbs of Paris, France, during the 1980s and 1990s. In time they came to refer to themselves as "Yamakasi," a word from the African Lingala language meaning "strong man, strong spirit." Central to this group were figures now known internationally through movies, documentaries, and other appearances in the world's media. They included such greats as Yann Hnautra, David Belle, and Chau Belle-Dinh.

The Yamakasi acquired a semi-mythical status within France, as they were regularly seen practicing their fledgling art form along cityscapes and street architecture of every imaginable kind. It was only a matter of time before local, then regional and national, news groups began reporting on this unusual and visually stunning activity, and the word Yamakasi soon became synonymous with breathtaking and seemingly high-risk stunts. In truth, the Yamakasi were discovering and refining a discipline of self-improvement that was far removed from anything as simple as adrenaline-seeking extreme sports.

A NEW IDEALISM

An unwritten code grew up between these men, a discipline founded on pushing their limits and seeking a way to reach anywhere they chose to go, no matter how difficult the path. They sought to challenge themselves in every conceivable manner and to be able to meet any task laid before them. Testing both mind and spirit was the ultimate aim, achieved through testing the body. From this need to master themselves and their environment, arose many of the movements and concepts that are the signatures of the discipline today. And so the art of displacement was born.

THE ART OF DISPLACEMENT

At its core, the art of displacement can be distilled to the elements of running, jumping, and climbing. However, that would be to describe the art, not to define it—which is something else entirely. Laurent Piemontesi, one of the founders, once equated it to "an art of living," meaning that it is a certain approach to life, rooted in self-reliance, independence of thought and action, inner strength and resolve, and being physically and mentally as complete a human being possible. The aim of this book is not to delve into such detail, however, but rather to provide a first touch of the art, a guide along its first steps. And for that we must, by necessity, concentrate on the body of the art, found in the daily training.

On the physical level, parkour aims to enable you to move freely through and over any terrain, in any conditions. In practice, it focuses on developing the fundamental attributes required for such movement—

There are a number of universally accepted terms for this practice.

L'art du déplacement: The first, and perhaps most accurate, name for the subject of this book was in French, and literally translates as "the art of displacement."

Parkour: Introduced by David Belle, one of the original practitioners, this term was first used in 1998. It derives from the French word *parcours* meaning "route" or "course."

Freerunning: The brainchild of Guillaume Pelletier, a representative of a group of French practitioners involved in the production of a Channel 4 documentary, *Jump London*, in 2003, this term was used in order to communicate this amazing new concept to an English-speaking audience.

balance, strength, dynamism, endurance, precision, spatial awareness, and creative vision. The discipline is a way of training your body and mind in order to be as completely functional, effective, and liberated as possible in the physical realm. It is also a way of thinking, based on rigorous self-discipline, autonomous action, and self-will.

This is a discipline of self-improvement on all levels, an art that reveals your physical and mental limits, while offering ways to overcome them. It is a return to a more natural way of moving and a method by which to unlock the enormous potential hidden within your anatomy and physiology. Very rarely do any of us achieve our full potential; modern, sedentary life has put to sleep much of our inherent physical power and vitality.

TRAINING

Parkour is a way to recapture your true potential, through a seemingly paradoxical combination of intense discipline and absolute freedom. Both are central tenets of the art of displacement, and it is only through such disciplined training that you can come to move so freely in your environment as well as within yourself.

You hold in your hands an introduction to this art, containing knowledge and experience that comes directly from the founders themselves. But a book can only ever be an introduction. This art has to be lived to be understood, and to live it you have to focus on what is both the means and the end of parkour—movement.

behind the jump

Getting started

Freerunning is not about perfecting set movements or achieving predefined goals. Nor is it about imitating the movements of others. It's about finding your own natural way to move, and then refining and improving that movement toward becoming proficient.

It is a good idea to acquire the basic elements of training and to master simple techniques in order to gain a strong and secure foundation. Without these vital basics in place, it will take much longer for you to be able to move safely and efficiently.

The aim of this book is to give you enough of an introduction to the training and core techniques of parkour to prepare you for the discipline of freerunning under the guidance of an experienced trainer. Once you can flow seamlessly from one movement to the next, you will have found parkour.

The book demonstrates some of the most fundamental movement areas in parkour, along with illustrated tutorials of certain techniques. Do not rush through the techniques in an effort to master them all in as short a time as possible. Instead, take your time. Concentrate on just one or two of the movement groups in each training session.

Allow yourself time to absorb the movements and how they feel. The aim is to become very comfortable with the basics and to progress from there. Once you understand how to use these techniques, you will start to apply them naturally across a variety of situations until you move fluidly.

The instruction given here has been distilled from the work of several founders and principal developers and instructors from France and the UK, whose methods of training have been tried and tested over many years.

" There is no substitute for regular, smart training. No shortcuts, no secrets. Practice well and often, and you'll get there. "

Anatomy of a freerunner

Your first question should be: How much do I know about my body? If the answer is "not very much," then it's time to learn. You don't need to become an expert, but you do need to have a basic understanding of your own anatomy—the major muscle groups, how the joints function, and what is good and bad for your body as a whole.

Parkour training will work most of the muscles in your body, particularly the quadriceps (thighs), gluteus muscles (butt), calf muscles (lower legs), biceps, triceps, deltoids, and pectorals (arms, shoulders, and chest), and the back and abdomen muscles (referred to here as the core muscles). It will also strengthen the other connective tissues of your body—the tendons and ligaments.

Tendons usually connect muscle to bone, while ligaments connect bone to bone. They take much longer than muscles to strengthen and become supple, which is why it is very important not to rush into doing powerful movements or big jumps when you begin training—your muscles may exert too much strain on your connective tissues, causing them to rip or tear, which can lead to serious physical damage. Progress slowly and allow your anatomy to develop the strength and resilience needed for parkour in its own time.

ANCIENT ANATOMY

One thing is for sure: our bodies were not designed for dropping, running, and generally bouncing around on concrete. Such hard surfaces did not even exist for most of our evolution. Technology, and therefore our living environment, has changed radically in the past few hundred years, while our bodies remain largely as they have been for the past tens of thousands of years. We are ancient anatomies inhabiting a digital age, and the result is a fairly serious incompatibility. The only way around this is to prepare and protect your anatomy through good, regular training and through proper understanding of how your body works. Take time to do some research into this area and you will not regret it.

>>> Discipline: the basics

The first thing to grasp when practicing the art of displacement is that this is not a series of techniques and set movements that you must master: rather it is about the development of six basic "elements," which, collectively, allow you to develop your own way of moving and your own physical and mental potential. You should apply these elements to your training as often and as regularly as possible, blending several of them into each session.

1 >RUNNING

For a practitioner of parkour, running is the basis of all movement. The running step—the approach—is used prior to the majority of dynamic actions and, for maintaining functional fitness and overall health, there are few better things than regular running. It is important to practice all types of running, from light jogging to distance running to sprinting. Do this, and the stability and surety of your steps will improve along with your power and fitness.

2 >JUMPING

Jumps come in huge variety, from standing to running jumps, single- to double-leg jumps, vaults, drops, arm jumps, and many more. All of them rely on the ability to push from the legs to clear a gap or obstacle of some sort. A strong jump also means a strong landing as, essentially, you use the same muscles for both jumping and landing. Jumping can help your drops, wall runs, vaults, and any other technique that requires, or benefits from, explosive power from the legs. The best training for a strong jump is quite simply to practice jumping as often as possible and in a wide variety of situations.

3 >CLIMBING

Climbing features in many movements, and develops your whole body strength in a highly functional fashion, particularly your grip and upper-body endurance. It is something we should do naturally and easily, but rarely practice in our everyday lives.

4 >BALANCE

Balance is a skill you learn like any other, and is something that requires constant practice and work. It is important to understand that you use balance in all movement, not just when walking or running on thin walls, ledges, and railings. Even when you jump, vault, and make landings you must maintain balance to avoid falling or losing control of the movement.

5 >STEALTH

Stealth means moving as quietly as possible, and is a fundamental principle in parkour training. It is important to understand that, in practicing silent movement, you are not just being quiet for quiet's sake: it has a purpose. And that purpose is to improve and refine your control over your physical ability. Moving silently means moving with absolute precision as well as with constant awareness of your body. Consider how much noise your footsteps and movements make; don't let each footfall clumsily strike the ground.

Being quiet when you move means your muscles are working more—not only giving you more control, but also training you to be more dynamic and powerful. Silence means you have control. Control means you can really begin to move.

6 >TOUCH/SENSITIVITY

In its simplest sense, "touch," in parkour, means one's physical sensitivity in movement, the ability to move with coordination, grace, and precision. Good touch is demonstrated by precise foot placement and soft contact with all surfaces. It means having good spatial awareness and control of your body in relation to the obstacles around you.

It also refers to your sense of connection with the environment through which you are passing, your "feel" for the surfaces and the shapes of the obstacles you are moving over. Good touch displays itself in a practitioner who takes fewer steps as he moves over terrain, demonstrating true economy of motion and greater fluidity.

The natural method of training

Parkour is a very natural method of training. You don't need hi-tech equipment, special clothing, or even dedicated training spaces or pitches. It simply involves you and your environment—and maybe a good pair of shoes. The aim of parkour is to take your natural movements and develop them to whole new levels.

A TRANSFORMATIVE PRACTICE

Parkour offers methods and approaches that have been pressure-tested and refined over many years to create an amazingly simple, but effective, way of training both your body and your mind. This is a true transformative discipline, in which you practice a set of physical movements regularly, with the intention of improving them and, at the same time, your inner self as well. Many of us never reach our full potential; too much is done for us in this modern age. This is a terrible waste, because our bodies are incredible and sophisticated tools, and can do the most unbelievable things.

FORGING THE BODY

To reach our full potential, we must break free of many limiting habits from our generally sedentary and unchallenging lifestyles. Our bodies are usually not ready for the strains and pressures of practicing such explosive movement, especially on the concrete and metal surfaces of the urban jungle. Any attempt to copy the high-powered actions performed by seasoned practitioners, without the necessary training and physical preparation, is to invite almost certain injury and long-term damage.

That's why a large proportion of training in parkour falls under the loose term, "conditioning"—the process of preparing the muscles, joints, connective tissues, and bones of the body for the demands of practicing the art. To be able to practice safely, and for as long as you wish, it is absolutely vital that you first develop the necessary physical attributes that underlie the movements.

The physical aim of parkour is to be as functionally fit, strong, and capable for as long as possible in life—to become the best version of yourself that you can—not to explode out of the blocks, have a few years of energetic practice, and then stop because of injury or overstraining of the body. Parkour is an art of living, a way of approaching not only your environment, but also your life.

This conditioning process is a way of forging your body to prepare it for the rigors of training. It creates a kind of "body armor" of muscle and toughened tissue that not only protects your whole anatomy from harm through repeated impacts, but also shields you if, and when, you fall or strike a surface unintentionally during a movement.

instruction from experienced and qualified teachers before embarking on a physical conditioning regime.

THE PHYSICAL BENEFITS

Good parkour training brings about incredibly positive physical changes, as it requires you to use your body as it was meant to be used; functionally and holistically. This training is far removed from linear isolations of muscles on a weights machine—freerunning tests all of the body all of the time, and almost every movement requires most of the major muscle groups to work together. However, attempting

> " Good parkour training will go some way to helping you reach your true potential and you will come to realize that your limits are far beyond what you could ever imagine. "

It is vital to understand that, even in conditioning, you must not rush or push too hard, too fast. Connective tissue such as tendons and ligaments take much longer to strengthen than muscles, and to overdevelop muscles without giving thought to the increased strain on the connective tissues invariably leads to repetitive-strain injuries such as tendonitis. Always seek proper

these movements without proper understanding of the art can lead to negative results for the body and less functionality.

This fine line between positive development and pushing the body too far is best negotiated under the guidance of a professional, until you become sensitive enough to your own body to be able to manage this balancing act alone.

>> THE BODY AS YOUR TOOL

A practitioner of parkour does not bring weights or clumsy machinery to his sessions: his body is his one and only tool. The principal practice for parkour is to repeat and refine the movements of parkour, improving tensile strength, flexibility, and coordination as you go, creating kinetic chains between the muscle groups while increasing neuromuscular efficiency.

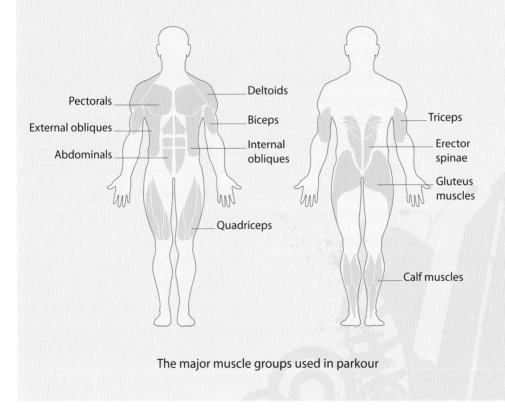

Pectorals

External obliques

Abdominals

Deltoids

Biceps

Internal obliques

Quadriceps

Triceps

Erector spinae

Gluteus muscles

Calf muscles

The major muscle groups used in parkour

Holistic health

Everything you do has an impact on your personal, mental, and physical development as you progress through life: how and what you eat, how you train, how you think, how you rest, how you work, and so on. All of these areas can either positively or negatively affect your overall health and abilities. The demands of parkour are such that you cannot separate how you practice from how you live.

Being healthy does not mean simply dropping a few training sessions into your week, however. Your body is a highly complicated and connected set of systems, and if one area is neglected, the rest will all suffer in turn. You have to start seeing yourself as a product of your lifestyle—because you are. It all comes down to finding a good balance between exercise, rest, proper nutrition, and enjoyment. Miss any one of those four, and you are not being healthy. Notice the last one: enjoyment. This is very important. If you don't enjoy your training and your lifestyle, you won't stick at it for long enough to gain from it.

The words "health" and "whole" come from the same root in language. To progress far in parkour, it is necessary to view your body and mind as a whole—to realize that you must care for your overall health in order to prepare you for the rigors of this art. Eat well, rest when you must, tend carefully to any injuries, and nurture a fresh mind and a strong spirit.

FUNCTIONAL FITNESS

To practice freerunning, you must become functionally strong and fit. For parkour, this means having a level of strength, agility, and cardiovascular fitness that enables you to move your own body weight over, under, or through any obstacles in your path. It is not the isolated muscular strength of weight lifting or the overly specialized physical development of a sprinter or distance runner. Rather, it is the ability to be fully capable within your environment at all times. The key is to focus on becoming functional in any given situation: to be able to move with speed, control, and coordination at all times.

The parkour environment

When you begin training in parkour, get ready to see the world in a whole new light. Quite simply, anyone who practices parkour, for even a short amount of time, soon finds that their perception of their environment undergoes a fairly radical overhaul. Walls, railings, buildings, barriers… structures of every shape and size cease to be seen as they were intended to be seen, and become, instead, components of a vast, almost limitless playground.

The training for parkour—the liberated approach to your surroundings, the hands-on interaction with your environment—develops a wider vision for the practitioner. Boundaries fall away, and structures built to contain become stepping-stones to greater physical and mental liberty. Strange things begin to happen… walls become nothing more than "vertical floors," for example, to be run up or along; metal handrails seem to morph into intricate pathways to be walked; gaps in architecture become spaces to be filled with dynamic jumps. Very swiftly you find yourself seeing city streets, squares, stairways, even simple sidewalks, as something quite different. Everywhere becomes an opportunity for movement, everything a training apparatus.

Yet it is important to understand that this "vision" comes only through practicing parkour—only once you have got hands-on with the structures of your urban environment, gauged distances for jumps, felt surfaces, been aware of drops and gaps—only then does your vision take in your surroundings in an entirely new way. Merely pondering these ideas intellectually does not bestow this "parkour vision." You have to practice it, to experience it—you have to live it.

Once you have this vision, you will begin to gain a new respect for the environment in which you live and train. Your aim when finishing training, therefore, should always be to leave an area in the same state as when you started. Only use objects and materials that you are sure you won't damage—this will also help to keep you safe as you move. The aim is to leave no trace. In doing so you will show respect for your environment and for others who live there.

02

movement

Parkour practice

The ideal way to practice parkour is to consider the core movements—running, jumping, climbing—and how you can build on these to develop seamless sequences as you move through the urban landscape. This is a highly physical discipline, however, and it is vital that you understand the "theory" of the movement—why you use and move your body in a certain way for a jump—before getting to grips with the "practice"—actually making that jump.

The following pages take you through each of the fundamental freerunning movements in turn, describing what that move is, how and when you should use it, and offering basic guidance on performing the move correctly, safely, and efficiently. In each case, there is at least one demonstration in the Tutorials section of the book (see pages 83–143), to help you when it comes to putting some of this theory into practice.

It is essential that you start by learning how to land from any sort of jump or drop, and how to use the roll in order to disperse the impact of landing in order to protect your body. These are core elements of parkour training, and you simply must take the time to learn them and learn them well. From here, you can tackle simple jumps, mounts, and vaults before moving on to the more dynamic wall runs, underbars, and tic-tacs.

As you work through the movements, remember, too, that the elements discussed in the first section of the book have a part to play, and that the principles of silence, coordination, spatial awareness, and balance apply to all aspects of parkour.

Always take the time to warm up and down properly before and after each session, and to observe the guidelines for practicing parkour safely and with the minimum risk of damage to your body.

Warming up

A good, thorough warm-up is an essential part of any training routine. It prepares both your body and mind for the rigors and demands of dynamic movement, greatly reducing the chance of injury while improving overall efficiency.

Warming up also greatly reduces the chance of incurring small, silly injuries from your training. These can be any number of things, from an overextension of a joint to pulled muscles or torn ligaments, and usually result from a lack of flexibility in the joint or muscles. Flexibility improves when your muscles and tendons are hot, so make sure you get warm and stay warm at all times during your training period.

Develop a warm-up routine that covers all the major muscle groups and joints—20 minutes minimum. This should get your internal temperature up to around the critical 102° Fahrenheit (39° Celsius) mark (see below). And if you need more time to get comfortably warm, just keep on warming up. Only you can know when you are fully ready to train.

>> BODYHEAT

Warming up is exactly that—a warming of the body. Its purpose is to raise your body temperature enough to create the ideal conditions for the smooth running of all the physical systems you are about to use.

At rest, the human body typically sits at between 97–98.5° Fahrenheit (36-37° Celsius). However, the optimal body temperature for physical activity is 102° Fahrenheit (39° Celsius), and those extra couple of degrees are extremely important. That slight rise in temperature has highly beneficial effects when it comes to the capability of the body to carry out extreme physical exertion.

> If you find your routines becoming mundane and boring, change them. Be creative, and you will find that you can enjoy the warm-up as much as you enjoy the training itself. "

> **Global warm-up:** Light exercise, such as slow running or skipping, to increase the heart rate slightly and raise your core temperature. This should result in a light sweat and an increased heart rate but should not tire you out. This gets the blood flowing freely, carrying oxygen to the muscles that are about to be used. Ten minutes should be enough, but you are the best judge of when you are feeling warm enough to begin.

> **Activity-specific warm-up:** Exercises that prepare the body systems and muscle groups that are to be most used during the training session. For parkour this means warming up most of the major muscle groups. This part of the warm-up should also involve dynamic stretching, joint rotations, and regulating your breathing.

ON ALL FOURS

There are plenty ways in which you can warm up. The key is to find one that safely and simply prepares your muscles as well as your coordination, balance, and spatial awareness.

One excellent method is known as "quadrupedal movement" (QM), and involves continuously moving around on all fours like an animal. A QM session should involve walking forward, backward, and sideways on only your hands and feet while being careful to be as quiet and as soft as possible, stretching the limbs and letting the body move naturally in all directions. You can add rolls along the ground, twist and turn your body, raise your hips so your arms and legs are straight, or go as flat as possible to get the upper-body muscles working.

This is a great way to warm up, because it involves all of the joints and muscle groups, but without putting them under any undue strain. It's safe, effective, complete, and can be a hard workout by itself. Vary the movements as much as possible for a good warm-up.

Warming down

A warm-down period should follow any demanding training session to encourage the muscles, ligaments, and organs to return to their natural length and position within the body. Stopping suddenly can interrupt your cardiac rhythm, reducing blood circulation to and from the heart, leaving you feeling faint after training. Bring the heart rate down slowly, however, and the cardiac rhythm will remain unbroken.

All muscular activity generates a toxin known as lactic acid. If not broken down, this will cause muscle aches for some time after training. To break it down, the muscles have to be working still, but at a lower intensity. Slow running, walking, and light skipping are all suitable for eliminating lactic acid.

A warm-down should take no less than 20 minutes. Drink lots of water to replenish lost fluids and help clean out toxins. Taking a shower also washes away those toxins from the body that result from sweating. Always allow your body to recover properly between sessions. After intense, anaerobic exercise, you really should take a good 24–48 hours rest to fully eliminate all toxins from the body.

>> STRETCHING

Stretching is a vital component of every warm-down. Work on all the major muscle groups, easing the tension out of them, employing gentle massage if necessary. Relax the muscles, tendons, and ligaments, and concentrate on slowing your breathing until it is deep and measured. Use the time to calm your mind and center your awareness, letting go of all the stress, anxieties, and fears that can accumulate during training. This is a time to re-integrate body and mind, so take as long as you need until you feel comfortable, relaxed, and physically light.

Safety

The most important aspect of good parkour training is your own safety. Just like any athletic discipline or sport, parkour has its risks. Injuries are never much fun, and worst of all they will greatly hinder your progress in training.

FIVE STEPS TO TRAINING SAFELY

1 >**Don't attempt too much, too quickly:** It takes time for the body to adjust to the demands of parkour, and to learn good coordination, and even the basic movements, properly.

2 >**Train your body first:** It is very important to develop the necessary muscle groups and strong connective tissue, such as tendons, before trying any movements that put a strain on the body. Put as much work into physical conditioning and functional strength as you do for movement skills.

3 >**Train at ground level:** Most training should be done at ground level, where the most interesting terrain can usually be found. Develop your skills at ground level, only trying things slightly higher up as you become more confident.

4 >**Check your training area:** Check surfaces to make sure they are solid, unbroken, and have a good grip for the movements you want to try. Take some time to check the floor for possible obstructions or dangers and clear them away if found.

5 >**Seek proper guidance:** Find a qualified instructor or an experienced practitioner to help guide you as you begin parkour. This will save you from making countless unnecessary errors in the early period of your training, thus making your practice more efficient and effective from the start. The rewards will be more than worth the effort of finding someone suitable to learn from.

>>> Landing

// **See** Tutorial: Straight landing, pages 86–87

Learning how to land from a drop, jump, vault, or indeed any other movement, is one of the first things you must focus on and it is important to get it right from the start.

THE IMPACT OF LANDING

Parkour is not about dropping from great heights. At times that may be necessary to complete a certain movement, but being able to do so does not make you a good, or better, practitioner. Dropping from any height onto a hard surface sends considerable shock through your body. It is vital to remember, therefore, that you must always land well.

>> IMPACT DAMAGE

The impact of a poor landing causes long-term damage to the skeleton, particularly ankle and knee joints, but also lower back and hips. Tendons and ligaments are also at risk from the added strains on the body.

SLOWLY BUT SURELY

The key to landing in the right way is to absorb and redistribute the impact of the shock in an effective manner.

Know your limits: The first thing to be aware of when you start training is that your body will not be ready for big drops of any nature, even if you feel that it is.

Practice makes perfect: Unless you practice landing techniques and movements over and over on small drops (certainly below your own head height) your body's systems will not learn to manage the impact in a safe way.

Build on your technique: Progress within the limits of what your body can safely absorb, and that will be different for each individual. With training and experience you will become more comfortable with your landings, until your body begins to do it instinctively every time. It is only at this stage that you will begin to feel safe and secure in all your movements.

LANDING BASICS

There are many different ways to land, depending on the movement you have just performed. The first thing to know is that landing well is not simply a matter of dropping from some height; it takes a great deal of time, practice, and the repetition of all kinds of landings—from jumps, vaults, drops, dives, and so on—before you can really know that you are not damaging yourself as you move across hard surfaces. Having said this, there are several points to consider if you want to land well, no matter what the movement.

> "It's all about knowing what you are doing. Don't just jump and crash into the floor, hoping your body can manage the impact; always land with purpose."

The following basic guidelines, if adhered to, will greatly improve the impact-absorption and quality of your landings, making you better able to tackle a much wider variety of training environments.

Quietness: The quieter the landing, the better it is. The more you use your muscles to absorb a landing, the more you spare your bones and joints from the shock. So aim to be as quiet and as soft as possible as your feet connect with the ground.

Alignment: To make the best use of your anatomy, you want to redistribute the impact over as many muscles, tissues, and physical levers as possible. To do this, those structures must be aligned correctly above each other. This means trying to keep both legs in the same position as each other.

Balls of the feet: Almost without exception, every single landing you make on your feet should be on the front part of the sole of the foot. Landing flat-footed, or on your heels, means you are unable to use the lever and muscles of the ankle and lower leg. This results in huge amounts of shock driving into the knees and lower back. Land on the balls of your feet, and you will initiate a chain reaction of muscles from the foot upward to absorb the impact. You also will have better balance and stability on landing.

Be relaxed: Don't lock your legs or upper body as you hit the floor. Most of your anatomy is elastic and, if allowed to relax, will absorb and redistribute the impact very well.

Muscle recruitment: Using more muscles to absorb the impact of a drop will spread the shock throughout those muscles and will considerably lessen the effect of the impact on your body. To do this, you have to teach your body to recruit chains of muscles rather than simply one or two isolated muscles. It takes time and repetition of the technique at low levels for the body to acquire this ability.

Breathe: Don't hold your breath as you land, especially on drops from height. Doing so causes you to become rigid and, therefore, unable to compress your body properly. Ideally, you should breathe out just as you hit the ground, in order to help your body relax and to absorb the shock.

Rolls *(roulade)*

// **See** Tutorial: Basic roll, pages 88–89

In parkour, the roll is something you simply cannot get by without. You use it to redirect the energy you generate on landing when dropping from a height. This means the energy is dispersed forward and outward rather than back up into your body. In much the same way as a parachutist rolls upon impact with the ground, this technique preserves your body from shock and damage, and enables you to drop from heights that would be otherwise unmanageable.

STRUCTURE OF THE ROLL

The roll technique is designed for use on any surface, hard or soft, and so protects the body and head as much as possible. The aim is to avoid rolling over any bony protrusions in the body and to use, as much as possible, your body's flesh and muscle to connect with the ground as you make contact. The technique itself is personal, like most movement in fact, and only you will know whether it is working well or not. Nevertheless, there is a certain, fundamental, structure to follow.

Significantly, this structure is very different than that of a traditional gymnastics roll. Primarily, you do not roll over your head and along your spine. (Doing this on hard surfaces can cause serious injury.) Instead, you should aim to roll diagonally, from one shoulder, down across your back to the opposite hip, coming up on the fleshy part of your buttock and the side of your leg.

This technique also allows you to come out of the roll directly into a running position and on the balls of your feet, so that you can continue to move fluidly without any pause for balance or orientation.

>> TIMING THE ROLL

Timing is absolutely everything with this technique, as a roll must begin immediately upon contact with the ground. The slightest hesitation, and the shock of the landing will have already gone back into your body.

ROLLING BASICS

The technique of the roll is not difficult, but making it work for you can take time and lots of practice. It has to be good, in order to avoid rolling on any bony parts of the body (shoulder bones, too much of the spine, hipbones, or the coccyx). Any of these connecting with the ground will cause you a lot of pain and prevent you from rolling well.

Collapse: The idea is to allow your legs to absorb the initial touch from the drop and then for your body to collapse forward into the roll in a controlled manner. Don't dive forward from a standing position, but let your legs collapse steadily, so that when you roll you are already close to the ground.

The roll: Once into the roll, you should have one side forward, probably your strong side. Touch the palms of your hands to the ground to create a tactile connection and also to protect yourself if anything goes wrong at this stage. Allow the momentum to carry you forward into the roll, over your forward shoulder, and diagonally across your back as you put your head to one side. You should not roll over your head at any time.

Stay round: Keep your legs tucked in tight beneath you—this is to make you smaller and rounder, and to avoid any flailing limbs from striking objects or the floor as you roll. Obviously round things roll very well, so make yourself as round as possible.

Coming out: Come out of the roll sideways, with your legs beneath you, and onto your toes not the tops of your feet. Coming out this way means you will not roll down the spine or onto the coccyx, but that the meaty part of your butt and side of your leg will connect with the ground, minimizing any pain. Immediately you have your feet beneath you, push forward and continue running.

STRIVING FOR PERFECTION

It will take practice and many small adjustments before your roll works every time and causes you no discomfort. Practice on your strong side first, but soon begin to work on both sides in order to be effective, no matter which side you come down on. When you crack it, you will be able to roll on any surface without pain and you will find yourself using this tool throughout your training to keep your body free of undue impact.

Standing jumps

// **See** Tutorials: Standing precision jump, pages 90–91; Staggered landing, pages 92–93

Central to many of the movements in parkour, jumps are recognized as a signature of the discipline. There are many situations in which the only way to reach a destination is to clear a gap or obstacle in one jump, and this is something you must get to grips with early on. There are different types of jump for a variety of situations, but all are explosive, fast, and controlled.

MUSCLE POWER

A standing jump is one that has no run-up to it. This is a whole-body movement that uses not only the legs, but also the core muscles and upper body, and a swing of the arms as you push off and stretch into the movement. It is essential to have strong leg and abdominal muscles for this.

The action of jumping puts a great deal of strain on these muscles and the connecting tendons and ligaments, especially when landing on hard surfaces like concrete and metal. You should not attempt long or difficult jumps from the start, therefore. Instead, the key is to repeat many small jumps, in order for your body to become accustomed to the action and to learn how to absorb the impact of the landings. In order to jump well, you must develop a good technique for takeoff and landing, and must learn to control the power of the jump.

> It can feel great to jump, but it must be practiced correctly and safely. With good training, you will be amazed at the distance you can cover without needing any run-up at all, simply from the coordinated, explosive power of your own body.

STANDING-JUMP BASICS

The best way to train your body for jumping is to jump—a lot! You don't necessarily need to practice very long or high jumps; you will build the right chains of muscles in the lower legs and the abdomen simply through many repetitions of jumps that are within your limits. The key is to concentrate on making each individual jump as perfect as possible.

Takeoff: You need a fast, explosive takeoff, good coordination while in flight, and a soft, controlled landing. Lean into the jump, and push as hard as you can with your legs. Always choose your landing spot before you jump and aim to land as precisely as possible.

In flight: Raise your knees during the jump, and extend your feet toward the landing area. This will give you more distance and a softer touchdown as you reach your destination. It will also help you clear any obstacles between you and where you intend to land.

Landing: Always bend your legs when landing (though not too deep a bend) to allow your muscles, rather than the skeleton or joints, to absorb the impact. Aim to be soft, quiet, and completely controlled on landing. Try not to wobble or overbalance as you come to a stop; control is everything.

TRAINING DRILLS

There are various drills to practice for jumping. These, in particular, will help develop a more controlled takeoff and landing.

Height jumps: Stand facing a low wall, perhaps 2–4 feet (60–120 centimeters) in height, and jump, legs together, from the ground onto the top of the wall. Turn round and jump off the wall to the ground, landing as lightly as possible in one spot. Repeat in sets of 10 jumps.

Clearance jumps: As for the previous drill, but this time, jump over the wall and land on both feet on the other side. Turn and jump back, again from a two-footed takeoff.

Length jumps: Find two points that you can jump between safely, and that are just within your maximum jump range. Push off from both feet and jump from one point to the other, concentrating on a good, controlled landing. Jump back to finish the drill, and repeat in sets of five.

Mounts

// **See** Tutorial: Corkscrew pop-up, pages 94–96

Parkour practice very often involves moving up and down as quickly as possible between different levels of terrain. Getting down from one level to another is managed by drops, turn vaults, and good landings; getting up high is covered by wall runs, climbing, and swinging.

IMPROVING POWER AND BALANCE

You can use simple mounts to improve explosive power and balance, simply by repeating the movements in sets of 10 repetitions on different obstacles. For example, taking hold of a handrail in both hands and popping up to land with both feet between your hands on the rail, works both the dynamic strength in your legs and your proprioceptive muscles as you balance and stand on the thin railing. You can then simply reverse the movement, under control, and repeat.

USING MOUNTS

Perhaps the most common level change is simply getting up onto a low wall or obstacle (below your own head height), and this is known as a mount. Although the movement may not appear to require attention or specific skill, the ability to get yourself onto such obstacles smoothly and efficiently will greatly improve your overall speed and versatilty as you cross any terrain.

Mounts enable you to get on top of an obstacle in one fluid motion, ready, then, to move in any direction from this new level. There are many variations, depending on the type of obstacle, the angle of approach, and where you want to move to once you are up.

MOUNT BASICS

When approaching a mount, the general principles are always the same: be quick, be soft, and be precise. You will find that getting very comfortable with even simple mounts greatly improves your overall confidence when moving over low-lying obstacles.

TRAINING DRILLS

Most of the simplest mounts can also be practiced as training drills. In general, it is safest to start on obstacles that are lower than your own waist height. Only once you have developed the necessary skills and confidence, should you progress to higher obstacles, staying below chest height.

The pop-up: You can perform this mount onto any flat-topped obstacle that is (usually) below chest height. It involves placing your hands flat on top of the obstacle and jumping up, and forward, to bring your feet onto the obstacle between your hands.

The movement is performed while running at the obstacle, to enable you to move directly on to the higher level without having to stop. It is best to land with one foot slightly in front of the other so that, as soon as your feet land on the surface, you can continue running in your chosen direction.

As a drill, stand in front of the obstacle and place both hands on top of it. Then, with one dynamic push, jump up to bring your feet between your hands so that you are crouched on top of the obstacle. Jump as quickly as you can and land as quietly as possible and always on the balls of your feet. It's important to raise your hips back and up as you jump, so that you create space for your legs to come beneath you. Step back down and repeat 10 repetitions in one set.

Corkscrew pop-up: This is a useful variation of the pop-up. By inverting one of your hands as you make contact with the obstacle, you can turn your body as you land, so changing the direction in which you are traveling.

Rail mounts: A more precise version of the pop-up is the same motion, but practiced on a handrail or thin, raised bar of some sort. This requires a lot more accuracy with the landing and good balance, so that you can then crouch on the bar or rail without falling forward or backward.

Extend the drill once you have popped up and are crouching on the rail, by then standing up slowly and under control. Stay there for a few seconds before slowly crouching down again, grabbing the rail, and stepping off backward. Repeat a few sets of this to work the proprioceptive stabilizer muscles in the lower legs and quadriceps as well as the core muscles. This will hugely improve your balance.

Sideways rail mounts: To increase the difficulty level slightly, pop up onto the rail while jumping sideways. To do this, place both hands on the railing, or bar, and pull with your arms to throw yourself up and to one side. Raise your hips and your knees and aim to land with both feet on the railing in a crouching position, still facing forward but 2–3 feet (60–90 centimeters) to one side of where you began. Practice on both sides to further improve your balance in movement and confidence in foot placement.

>>> Vaults *(passement)*

// **See** Tutorials: Step vault, pages 97–99; Turn vault, pages 100–102

Vaults offer a quick way of passing obstacles up to roughly your own chest height without breaking stride. Known as *passement* in French, vaults involve diving over an obstacle while placing one, or both, hands on it for balance, control, and extra power. Common obstacles to vault are low walls, handrails, tables—anything low enough to clear in one movement. A few rules apply:

Approach: Maintain momentum as you approach the obstacle, making the last few steps dynamic and light, so that you carry the speed of your approach into the vault.

Takeoff: Do not take off too close to the obstacle—if you do, you will be forced to jump upward more than forward, which will slow the entire movement down. Practice jumping at the obstacle from a little farther away as you run up to it, and you will find you are carried over it with less effort.

Hand placement: Make sure your hands are placed firmly on the obstacle as you pass over it. If you are vaulting a railing, make sure you get a good grip to maintain stability during your movement.

Exit: Aim to land on one foot so that you can immediately continue moving on your way.

Drills: The best way to train for vaults is to find an obstacle you can clear without too much effort, and to repeat the basic technique as often as possible. Allow the movement to become as natural as possible, with little energy expended as you go over the obstacle.

> " The key to passing obstacles with speed and fluidity is in a good approach and exit. Combine these with a good technique, and you will soon be flowing over your terrain with ease. "

Balance *(equilibre)*

The ability to maintain proper balance at all times in movement is a fundamental aspect of good parkour practice: it is vital for precision landings, crucial for moving swiftly on narrow surfaces, and critical for the proper execution of every type of vault. Having good balance and a refined sense of body position is of great benefit to the freerunner, and is essential for preventing falls.

Good balance is dependent on many different factors, some of which are biological, and almost all of these can be improved. As well as being dependent on our visual systems and the workings of the inner ear, balance is also a product of proprioception, the body's ability to orient itself in space without relying on visual or auditory stimuli.

Primarily, our ability to balance, and stay upright in any given situation, relies on a number of factors, involving the visual, auditory, and musculoskeletal systems. Visual signals are sent to the brain about the body's position in relation to its surroundings. These signals are processed by the brain, and compared to information from the vestibular and the musculoskeletal systems. Within the inner ear, a complex series of tubes, fluids, and sensitive hairs works to help the brain detect our body's movement and position, including perceptions of up and down, side to side, and circular movements. Taken together, these various and continuous streams of information enable us to maintain and regulate very precise balance, even during movement of any kind.

PROPRIOCEPTION

Proprioception requires the constant, accurate assessment of the body's position in space, and is facilitated by the contraction of numerous small stabilizer muscles as they make tiny adjustments to regulate balance. Balance is as much about effective and efficient recovery from imbalance as anything else. Using these muscles over and over again improves our general ability to make these constant slight corrections in balance, and so a broad variety of types of movement will produce the best results.

BALANCE BASICS

A practitioner of parkour must learn to balance and move on rails of all dimensions, on walls and miscellaneous obstacles of varying thickness and angles of inclination, and on surfaces of widely differing grip and traction. He must be able to shift the balance of his body weight as he vaults over barriers and fences. To be proficient, he must be able to maintain and control his balance and orientation while in midair to enable a safe landing from vaults, drops, and other jumps.

TRAINING DRILLS

By incorporating some, or all, of the following drills into your training program you will, over time, bring profound improvements to both your balance and your parkour.

Slow crouch: This is a simple, yet very effective exercise for static balance, which can be performed anywhere. Standing with legs shoulder-width apart and body relaxed, raise yourself up onto the balls of your feet and then slowly crouch down until you feel your butt touch your heels. Hold for five seconds

" **Balance underlies everything we do in parkour, and simply cannot be practiced enough. With good balance, all other movements become much easier, and much safer.** "

Good balance is a skill you can develop almost all of the time, wherever you are, and whatever you are doing. When out walking, keep an eye open for raised curbs or low railings you can walk along instead of using the sidewalk. Even if there are no obstacles within sight, a few slow crouches done regularly will begin to add up.

Every training session should include some balance work, as this aspect of the discipline is so very fundamental to parkour.

then stand up slowly, still positioned on the balls of your feet. Repeat the exercise for sets of five. Slow crouches like this help to develop the leg muscles while engaging the stabilizer muscles around the lower leg to maintain the poised ball-of-the-foot stance.

Rail crouch: These are exactly the same as slow crouches, but performed on a solid horizontal railing. Practice the exercise first, standing perpendicular to the railing, and then in line with the railing to access different muscle groups of the legs. As your balance improves, increase the length of time in the crouch to 10 seconds.

Rail walking: Practice walking along railings of varying width and material, until you are comfortable with even thin, round railings. Learn to walk with your feet in line with the rail, and maintain proper control during every step. Be precise with your movements, and try to minimize sway. For extra difficulty, stop to add in some crouches along the way.

Post hops: Stand atop a solid post on one leg. Then, in one swift motion, swap feet in place so that you are standing on the other leg in exactly the same spot. Keep the knees slightly bent when doing this, and sink your weight down into your foot. The weight should be over the ball of the foot at all times. Try this exercise on posts of varying width and height, until you are comfortable. If you can find several posts in a row and close enough together, practice walking across them with small jumps, taking off and landing on one foot whenever possible.

Cat balance (*quadrupedie*): This is the practice of moving along a thin object—commonly a metal railing a few feet above the ground—on all fours. The act of keeping yourself in balance in this way works many of the muscle groups in the body, not only the hands, forearms, and legs but also the core muscles, the shoulders, and back. It's a great exercise to improve your proprioception and your whole-body strength.

Find a solid railing, or thin wall, and take a good grip before moving one foot at a time on to the top. You should be stretched out on the object with your weight equally distributed between your arms and your legs. Always climb carefully and establish a strong position on the railing before you attempt to move forward. Move your rear arm ahead of your front arm and then your rear leg ahead of your front leg, keeping your back parallel to the rail and your hips low. Take regular breaks to stretch the legs, as this activity places a small strain on the quadriceps muscles.

The aim is to be able to move swiftly and continuously along the rail. Once you are confident with the basic drill, be creative and find other ways to stretch yourself and make the drill harder for yourself.

Wall runs *(passe muraille)*

// **See** Tutorials: Wall run, pages 103–105; Pop vault, pages 106–108

P*asse muraille* literally translates from the French as "passing a wall," and this is precisely what it entails. Known commonly in freerunning as a wall run, this movement is used for getting up and over walls or obstacles that are too high to vault or jump. It requires a great deal of power in the legs and a highly coordinated movement of lower and upper body.

The aim is to transform your momentum going forward as you run at a wall, into energy that drives you up the wall when you reach it. In a sense, the aim is indeed to "run" up the wall. Stretching up with your hands, as soon as they reach the top of the wall or obstacle, you engage the muscles of the upper body, particularly your back, shoulders, and arms, to pull yourself onto the top of the wall and finish the movement.

A good wall run can carry you up walls that are easily over twice your own height, and which are otherwise absolutely insurmountable. It is a core technique in parkour and you will use it very often during movement and training, so it requires a lot of work from the start.

USING MOMENTUM

The key to getting this movement right is in generating and using the momentum properly, for it is the momentum from the run-up that you redirect into energy to carry you up the wall with one powerful motion. If the redirection of the momentum is slow or broken, you will not get much height and will likely end up dropping back down to the foot of the wall again.

THE REACH

One of the core principles of parkour is "to reach." Nothing better exemplifies this principle than the dynamic *passe muraille*, which enables you to reach places that would normally be far beyond your grasp. When the technique becomes something natural and instinctive for you, you will find yourself looking at walls not as walls but as "vertical floors" in a sense—something you can quite easily "run" up.

WALL-RUN BASICS

The movement of a wall run seems simple enough. You run at the wall and when about one stride from it, you jump slightly, placing the foot of your strongest leg against the wall at around waist height, and then push upward from that leg while extending both arms above your head to reach for the top. Easy in principle, yes, but in practice there are several key points that need to be perfected before you can achieve an explosive wall run.

Approach: It is vital to use good, long strides as you approach the wall. Stuttering as you near it will kill your momentum and leave you with nothing to put into the technique as you reach the obstacle. The critical steps are the last one before you hit the wall and the step you take on the wall itself. Both of these need to be dynamic, powerful, and well positioned.

Distance: You need to get the distance right when you take your final running step and jump at the wall. You should be about a running stride's distance from the wall as you begin the technique, so that you can place your foot waist height or above on the surface of it. Too close, and you will not be able to push up owing to the leg being too bent; too far away, and your momentum will leave you stepping too low on the wall, which takes away the energy of the approach.

Direction: When you push off from the wall, push up and not away or backward. To give yourself the best chance of reaching the top of a high wall, you must redirect the energy of your approach into vertical power. Getting your foot placement at the right height will make it easier to push up.

"The goal of the *passe muraille* is to reach the top of high obstacles in your path, which means you have to be thinking "up"!"

Coordination: It is important to be reaching with the whole of your upper body and arms as soon as you have pushed up from your leg. Too long a pause, and you will be dropping down as you reach up, which will not enable you to get very high. Maximize the push by coordinating the reach as you push up.

Strength: The speed of the final part of the wall run is dependent on the strength and power of your shoulders, back, and arms. This is the moment you pull your whole body up and over the lip of the wall or obstacle—often from a straight hanging position if you have had to reach during the technique. This is known as the "climb-up," and the best way to develop the strength is simply to practice the movement over and over again. Try to make it as fast as possible, so that you have a dynamic climb-up and can quickly get your feet to the top of the wall.

TRAINING
Start with walls that you can manage with a medium amount of effort until the technique feels comfortable, then begin trying for the tops of obstacles that are at the limit of your reach as you push. You will find that you can tackle very high obstacles while reaching with just one arm, as this allows more flexibility in your upper body. If you do this, try to get the other arm to the top as quickly as possible to enable a fast climb-up.

Once you are proficient at wall runs, and confident in your ability to perform the movement, you can move on to a pop vault, which allows you to clear the wall without having to touch your feet to the top of it as you pass over.

STAY FOCUSED
Whatever you do, try not to get too hung up on any individual element of training—always practice a movement as naturally as possible, as one fluid technique. If one aspect is weak and holding the fluidity back, break it down and work on it, but always come back to the whole movement.

Clearing *(franchissement)*

// **See** Tutorials: Spiral underbar, pages 109–111; Feet-first underbar, pages 112–114

The French term *franchissement* means to clear or cross an obstacle, and is used to describe a variety of movements that are not regular jumps or vaults, but that carry you through, under, or around something in your path. We sometimes group these movements together in the term "underbars," which refers to diving or pulling yourself beneath a bar, or through a small area, in one fluid motion. These can be feet-first movements, or you can lead with your arms and upper body; the point is always to find a way of moving through tricky obstacles without stopping.

Obstacles that you encounter in parkour will likely be varied, depending on where you go. This means the potential techniques for moving through any given terrain have to be limitless, too. You may have to create entirely new movements to deal with a new or unusual obstacle, and that is a very important skill to practice.

The key is to adapt. Be flexible with your movement. Try not to think in terms of set techniques, but learn to let your body instinctively find a way through, or under, or around… The core principles of being fluid, being fast, and being direct always apply. Spatial awareness, balance, and dynamism should be present in everything you do, no matter what type of movement it is.

Having said this, there are some optimum methods of *franchissement* that are widely applied, on account of their effectiveness and versatility.

UNDERBARS

These techniques are most often used for going between two horizontal objects that create a gap—handrails, stair railings, branches, fencing, and so on. They all involve gripping the object, usually the higher one, and controlling the movement with upper-body strength as you pass through the gap. A great way to warm up and work out, underbars work all the major muscle groups, especially the core muscles, as you must closely guide your whole body through gaps that are often not much bigger than yourself.

Drop jumps *(saut de fond)*

// **See** Tutorial: Forward drop, pages 115–117

Big drops have always been one of the spectacles of parkour, and the media loves to focus on this kind of movement, because of its seemingly superhuman nature. To be able to drop from a great height and walk away without injury demonstrates how parkour pushes the limits of human potential, maximizing on the capabilities of the human body.

For practitioners of the discipline, the drop jump is just another part of the overall goal of movement and is no more or less difficult than any other technique. Once you have got the hang of the principles, and the methods that keep you and your body safe while dropping, it is relatively simple and, in fact, soon becomes quite familiar.

It is very important to understand that you can only reach this level of comfort when performing drops through a considerable amount of regular training and conditioning. Dropping from anywhere above your own height puts enormous stress on your joints and connective tissues, and can cause serious, long-term damage if done without the correct preparations over months—even years—of dedicated training.

You may find when you begin training that you can drop from quite high without feeling pain or discomfort. Don't be fooled. If your body is not prepared, your muscles and connective tissues not resilient enough, and your technique inadequate, you will do irreparable harm to your joints and skeleton (see also, page 36).

However, if you train correctly and safely, taking your time to condition your body, you will find that you are, in fact, able to manage drops from height without doing any damage to your body.

> **Our bodies are "superhuman" or, at least, capable of far more than we usually imagine.**

DROP-JUMP BASICS

The secret of this movement is in the name: "drop jump." There is a huge difference between falling, which is uncontrolled descent, and dropping, which is controlled. In parkour you are always choosing to drop, and therefore this should be a movement that you know you are capable of performing and one that will not cause you harm. You must always work with whatever feels within your physical limits.

Landing: Good technique is everything. Every landing should be made on the balls of the feet first, letting the chain of muscles in the lower legs spread the impact up through the ankles, calf muscles, and quadriceps. This chain has to work very efficiently, and the best way to train it is to work the movement over and over from smaller jumps. (See also, Landing, pages 36–39.)

Intent: Your intention is very important. You should always aim to drop and land with purpose, so that you are controlling the descent, your body position, and your landing at all times. Pick your landing spot, be precise, and maintain your focus throughout the whole dropping motion.

Stay relaxed: Too rigid, and your suspension systems will not work properly, causing you damage. But too soft, and your alignment will be wrong and your body will simply collapse as you reach the ground. You are looking for a "relaxed firmness" throughout your body, like a coiled spring.

The importance of the roll: This cannot be overstated. Rolling, to redirect your downward energy away from your body, is vital on any drop that is too high for your leg muscles to be able to handle safely. Even if you do feel that you can manage the drop, and if there is space to roll, it is wiser to roll anyway just to minimize the impact even further. Do not neglect your roll (see also, Rolls pages 40–42).

ALIGNMENT

The body is a series of levers and joints that are very good at working together to absorb shock and redistribute unwanted energy from impacts, but it has to be aligned well to allow this to happen. For drops this means having the feet squarely beneath, and in line with, the knees and the knees beneath, and in line with, the hips. The upper body, too, should be aligned with the direction in which the hips are facing to prevent back injury. This alignment will allow your anatomy to work as it should in absorbing and redistributing impact across all the major muscle groups.

The alignment of your joints when you land from drops is very important. A misalignment somewhere, such as the knee to one side or a foot too far out to the side, can result in too much strain being placed on the joints above and below the misaligned area and this can lead to a sudden impact injury.

TRAINING DRILLS

The first thing to do is to strengthen and condition the muscles and connective tissues of the legs. In fact, this training will strengthen the whole body and especially the core, but the legs are what you should focus on as they will manage most of the impact.

Drops: Once your legs are feeling very solid and strong, and you are comfortable with drops from up to head height, you can begin practicing drops from slightly higher up. However, with these, you should complete fewer repetitions in each set, and there is no need to do sessions like this too often.

With good, incremental training, you can develop the ability to drop safely from surprising heights. You can also start to tackle, forward drops—where the movement

> **Your body must be ready to compress to absorb the impact, yet firm enough to hold your structure and your shape.**

Squats: Repeating simple squat drills—going from a standing position down to a full crouch and back up again—can also help strengthen the muscles around the knee joint, which is critical to protect.

Jumps: Begin with jumps down from 2–3 feet (a meter) high, and slowly increase the height over weeks and months so that your legs get used to the movement and learn how to absorb the shock. Repeat in sets of 10 and do as many sets as you feel give you a good workout without overstraining the muscles.

involves a forward as well as a downward motion. But this is dependent on doing that training and sticking to it. Parkour is an activity to be practiced for life, not just for a few months or years, and is about improving your movement and becoming more functional. Injuries and strains on joints only lead to less functionality. Be smart, and work hard to develop the physical and technical attributes you need in order to carry out this kind of movement successfully.

Stepping movements *(tic-tac)*

// **See** Tutorials: Tic-tac, pages 118–119; 360 tic-tac, pages 120–121

As you begin to practice freerunning, you will find that you view your surroundings in a radically different way. You will come to see obstacles as opportunities for movements, barriers as gateways, and new surfaces you never even noticed before. The tic-tac is a prime example of this altered perspective in action: effectively the movement involves stepping on a vertical surface and pushing from it onto, or over, other objects. You will find that you are quite capable of using walls like floors, providing you get the technique right.

It's all about body positioning and the angle at which you strike the wall. The better you become at gauging how this should be done in any given situation, the more you will find that you can pretty much kick off, or step from, any object to, or over, another. You can tic-tac from walls, rails, lampposts, bollards—in fact almost any street furniture you encounter, as long as it is solid enough and has a reasonable grip to the surface.

FLEXIBILITY AND FLUIDITY

This is one of those techniques that is extremely versatile and flexible, and one that you can use in countless scenarios to aid your movement and improve your creativity.

Tic-tacs are great to use in combination with other parkour techniques, including vaults (see pages 50–51) and precision jumps (see pages 90–91). For example, a tic-tac from a wall over a very high railing might be easier if you use your hand on the obstacle as you go, creating a tic-tac-to-vault combination. Or any tic-tac that requires you to land on a slim or small surface area, is working your precision at the same time.

> **Always think creatively with this type of movement and you will find endless variations to challenge you over and over.**

TIC-TAC BASICS

While there is huge variety within the tic-tac family of movements, there are certain principles that generally apply throughout, and that will help you get to grips with the technique to start with.

Position: Don't get too close to the wall, or object you are going to tic-tac from, before you take off into the move. If you are too close, your leg will bunch up on impact and it will take much more effort to straighten the leg will be able to jump away from the obstacle as you exit the move.

Pushing off: Aim to push up, as well as away, from the wall. This will give you more height, and therefore more distance, as you jump to, or over, the next obstacle. To facilitate this, make sure your foot is placed with the toes pointing roughly upward on the wall. If the toes point to the side or down, you will only jump horizontally at best and not make much distance as a result.

> When you become proficient at the tic-tac, it can often look as if you actually are running along a wall, defying gravity.

and push away. You are trying to step, or bounce, off the object quickly and with dynamism: aim only to have the briefest contact with the obstacle as you tic-tac.

Footing: The position of your foot on the wall, or object, is very important. Place the ball of your foot on the wall above your own waist height but below your shoulder height. This area is the best for being able to generate power while helping you get height for the jump. Generally speaking, the higher you can get your foot within this field, the farther you

Direction: As you push from the first obstacle, make sure you turn your body quickly to face the way you want to go. This will enable you to push in that direction and so reach your destination. Turning your head first will force your body to follow, and also allows you more time in which to site your landing.

Landing: As you are in the air, raise your knees: this will enable you to jump higher and get your feet to higher obstacles—this is essential if you are planning to land a precision jump from the tic-tac.

MULTIPLE STEPS

Of course, a tic-tac does not have to be just one step. Sometimes it helps to take two steps or more on the object, either to help you gain height or to cover distance horizontally. A common use of two steps is to tic-tac from a wall or obstacle and turn 180 degrees to reach an obstacle directly behind you. Two steps on the wall can give you a great base of height from which to push.

If space is limited, more steps on the wall can act as your run-up and help you generate momentum in a tight area. The key to being able to get more steps on a vertical surface is to have a good body position (which means one that is not too upright, which will make you simply slide down the wall on your first step) and to use swift, dynamic steps on the wall.

Advanced vaults

// **See** Tutorials: *Saut de chat*, pages 122–124; Lateral vault, pages 125–127

As demonstrated earlier (see pages 50–51), vaults are perhaps the most efficient way in which to move over and beyond any midsize obstacles in your path. Dynamic, fluid, and fast, a good vault should not interrupt your running. Different vault techniques are used for different situations—some to clear very wide obstacles, others to connect a series of movements, others still for pure speed and directness.

THE NEED FOR PRACTICE

The aim with all *passement* is to be able to use whatever type of vault you need without having to stop to think about it. The movements must become instinctive and natural: this only comes through practice and repetition, so drill the movements until you are totally proficient.

Also, while you will find certain vaults work better for you on certain types of obstacles—a *saut de chat* on walls rather than over railings (see pages 122–124)—the aim is to become functional with your movement in general. This means you should be able to use whatever vault feels natural and is effective for whatever situation you find yourself in.

When you begin, you will almost certainly favor one side over the other, but aim to practice all movements on both sides. To be functional you must be able to move equally well over obstacles to your left and right, without pause. When you can vault well, you will begin to see obstacles in your path as nothing more than stepping stones to move over, train on, and have fun with. How you view your surroundings will change radically, and you will begin to see paths of movement everywhere.

" The *saut de chat* requires confidence and a good spring but once mastered is an extremely natural and useful maneuver. "

ADVANCED-VAULT BASICS

To make your vaults dynamic and fast you need to develop a powerful chain of muscles and connective tissue in the lower legs. A great drill for developing this kind of explosive power is to bounce up and down repeatedly on the balls of your feet, reaching up to touch a fixed point a few feet above your head each time, perhaps against a wall. Do not bend your knees deeply on each landing and aim to bounce back up as quickly as possible, minimizing contact time with the ground.

SAUT DE CHAT

The *Saut de chat*, literally "jump of the cat" in French, has become known as the "monkey" or "kong vault", and is one of the most recognizable movements in freerunning, and is also highly useful in a number of situations. More of a controlled dive than a vault, the aim is to throw yourself over an obstacle headfirst, while placing both hands on its surface to control yourself and add momentum. Your legs then pass through your arms as you push off from the obstacle, allowing you to make good distance beyond it and keep moving.

LATERAL VAULT

The lateral vault involves jumping off one leg while swinging the other (usually outside) leg in front of you over the obstacle, and placing the hand nearest the obstacle on top of it for support. The trailing leg then tucks up beneath you to allow you to "slide" over the obstacle and keep moving. As you pass over, your second hand can be used on the obstacle to provide support, balance, and power as you exit. The shifting of weight from one supporting hand to the other during the movement means it can eventually be used on obstacles up to your own head height.

REVERSE VAULT

The reverse vault is a great technique for linking a series of movements over several obstacles. The vault gets its name from the fact that you actually throw yourself, in reverse, over an obstacle, spinning as you go to land facing the right direction for moving forward. It can be used in situations where there is little space to develop momentum, or where you have landed from a prior move and now have your back, or side, to an obstacle you want to pass.

Running jumps

// **See** Tutorial: Crane jump, pages 128–130

Parkour can be broken down, at the most basic level, to three movement areas: running, jumping, and climbing. Of these, running and jumping are, perhaps, the most common—and so the running jump is arguably the most fundamental movement in parkour practice. Certainly it is one of the most useful.

WHEN TO USE A RUNNING JUMP

A running jump is any jump for which you use a run-up to generate enough momentum to make the distance. Obviously, with a running jump, you can cover much greater distances than from a standing start, and this extra power is both a blessing and a challenge: because controlling the landing becomes that much harder when you have so much more momentum in the jump. And if the jump requires you to land on a thin wall or railing or in a very small area, you must be able to control your landing with great precision and stability, or you will not be able to perform the movement safely.

The movement involves considerable power and momentum and it is vital to build up to the longer jumps so that you can develop overall control and the muscular capability necessary for absorbing and managing the force that is generated by landing at the other end. The best way to do this, as with the standing jump, is to repeat running jumps that are well within your maximum range until your legs are prepared for the strains of longer jumps.

" It gives you a great feeling to use this type of movement, to really let go and put all your power and speed into one explosive leap. "

RUNNING-JUMP BASICS

The standard running jump is most commonly used to cross gaps or obstacles that are not suitable for moving on, or sometimes simply to hurdle an obstacle in your path, or to jump directly onto an object higher than ground level so that you can move along it. Whatever the use, the principle is always the same.

Run-up: The run-up should use measured and consistent strides, be fast, dynamic, and with every step on the balls of the feet.

Takeoff: The optimum angle of elevation when jumping is 45 degrees, so try to get this spot on. When you do, you will know.

Drills: Find a jump that is just within your maximum range and repeat it in sets until you are comfortable. Then increase the distance. Think roughly in terms of sets of 10 jumps, maybe doing just two or three sets to begin with. This will take a lot out of your legs, so if you feel sore and tired the following day, rest and let your muscles recover and rebuild.

Alternate your takeoff leg: You may begin by having a preferred leg to jump from, but you should train both sides equally. When you are drilling jumps, remember to alternate your takeoff leg. This way, both legs will develop good power and control.

RUNNING PRECISION JUMP

A running precision jump requires you to land on a thin, or small, object and to control that landing—sometimes called "sticking" the jump. It can take a lot of practice to get right.

The key is to aim for a little more height as you jump, so that you can come down onto the obstacle rather than hit it purely with horizontal momentum. Coming down onto an object makes it easier to stop and control yourself, and also gives you a better chance of balancing on the obstacle once you have landed. Aim to be soft as always, and use the balls of your feet for the landing.

CRANE JUMP

This jump is used where you cannot quite jump directly onto the top of an obstacle in one movement. You use the running jump as normal but then aim to get one foot only to the top of the obstacle, with the other leg left beneath you to balance you as you land.

In only trying to get one leg up to the landing, you are able to maximize the use of the hips and reach higher up with that one foot. This enables you to jump straight onto obstacles that you could otherwise not be able reach so directly.

Arm jumps *(saut de bras)*

// **See** Tutorials: Running arm jump, pages 131–133; Cat-to-cat, pages 134–135

The arm jump or *saut de bras*, known popularly as the "cat leap," is one of the easiest and, at the same time, one of the most difficult maneuvers to perform in parkour. The term covers any jump in which you land with your arms gripping the edge, top, or sides of an obstacle, with your feet against its vertical surface. Typically, the movement is completed by then pulling yourself up onto the top of the obstacle.

MAKING THE LEAP

Most commonly used to jump across a gap to a wall that is too high, or too far, to get your feet on top of directly, the cat leap allows you to cross terrain that is impassable in any other way. It's a truly functional movement that requires all of the major muscle groups to be able to perform.

Cat leaps can be used in many different situations, with the landing area often dictating the kind of body position and type of grip you will have to land with. The standard is a jump to a straight wall directly across from your takeoff, in which your feet and hands land on the wall at roughly the same time—your hands on the edge of it with legs bunched beneath you and your feet against the vertical surface for grip and absorption. A good cat leap has you landing fairly softly against the wall and absorbing the impact with the muscles of the whole body, and then using that stored elastic energy to pull yourself up onto the top of the wall.

Cat leaps can be done from a standing or running jump, or even from one cat leap to another by pushing off the wall you have just landed on and jumping for another—known as a *retour de bras*, or "cat-to-cat."

As with all jumps in parkour, it is advisable to start small, to let your body get used to the movement, and, over time, to develop the right strength and resilience in your muscles and connective tissues to be able to repeat longer cat leaps in due course.

ARM-JUMP BASICS

There is great variety in the uses of the arm jump and the techniques that can be applied to differing terrain.

STANDING ARM JUMP

The standing arm jump gives you time to focus on your landing area, calm your breathing, and build up to the leap. It is also unlikely you will jump with too much force from a standing start, so it is easier to land softly against the wall and control the landing.

To start with, find a wall that has a good grip and isn't too rough. It's important when drilling this move to end the cat leap by pulling yourself up onto the wall you have jumped to: this gets your body into the habit of doing so, building the strength to complete the movement in a fast and efficient manner.

RUNNING ARM JUMP

The running arm jump is used to cross long gaps or reach the edge of obstacles that are too high to jump straight onto. The major difference from the standing version is that you come into the wall with much more speed and energy, and therefore your grip and landing must be that much stronger and better. There is a fair amount of impact on landing this movement. You will have less time to gauge the distance and calculate the landing, so begin with jumps well within your range and slowly build up to longer ones as you become more confident.

LEVEL-TO-LEVEL ARM JUMP

This is an arm jump where the destination is at the same height or below the takeoff point, so you have to drop into the landing rather than jump straight across or up. This kind of cat leap is harder because of this, as gravity works with your weight to increase considerably the impact of the landing. If you are not suitably strong, you run the risk of not being able to hold on. One method of absorbing the impact is to allow your legs to hit the wall and then slide down it, prolonging the process of landing and leaving you hanging straight against the wall. This makes the climb-up harder as you no longer have your legs against the wall to push up from, but on long level-to-level arm jumps it can make the difference between staying on the wall and slipping off.

CAT-TO-CAT (*RETOUR DE BRAS*)

This is a great technique for developing coordination in the air and explosive power. The aim is to start from the cat-leap position against an obstacle, and push dynamically up and away from the wall while turning to land a cat-leap on a wall behind you or to one side.

Swings and hanging movements *(laché)*

// **See** Tutorial: Swinging *laché*, pages 136–137

The French verb *lacher* means, literally, "to let go," and is associated in parkour with all movements that involve you hanging by your arms from a bar, branch, or any horizontal object above you and then letting go of it—often with a swinging motion—to reach another object either with your arms or legs.

Simply suspending yourself in this way is very good training for the upper body and will stretch your joints, muscles, and connective tissues into a natural alignment, which can improve your posture and overall suppleness. Hanging (*pendu* in French) is in fact also a very useful physical conditioning exercise and should be practiced regularly anyway, to strengthen the arms, shoulders, upper back, and grip.

MONKEY MENTORS

To get an idea of what you are aiming for with *laché* movements, just watch the actions of monkeys and primates when swinging through trees. The strength and grace of these animals is an example to us all and, with training and commitment, you will find that the human body is capable of very similar movements, if not quite as powerful.

> **The most important attributes for this kind of activity are strong, supple arms and shoulders, and a good firm grip.**

SWINGING BASICS

The key to all *laché* movements, is to use your whole body as much as possible. Relying on your arms alone, leaving the core and legs as dead weight, will tire you out very quickly and you will never get very far.

STRAIGHT *LACHÉ*

This simple *laché* involves hanging from one horizontal object, such as a branch or bar, and dropping, under control, to catch another horizontal object below, using only the arms. The movement requires you to absorb the weight of the drop with your upper body, mainly the arms and shoulders. You should begin by dropping only a short distance—a foot or two (30–60 centimeters) maximum—to allow your body to get used to the technique and the suddenness of the catch.

Don't lock your arms too much as you catch the object below, or you will lose the absorption capabilities of your muscles. Don't be too limp with the arms either, or you will not be able to maintain your grip as you catch the object, owing to your falling body weight.

To repeat, reach up for the top horizontal with one arm at a time so that you are back in the starting position, and drop again. Practice with small sets of five repetitions to begin with. Don't overtrain, as it puts a lot of strain on the connective tissue of the wrists, elbows, and shoulders.

SWINGING *LACHÉ*

The most dynamic and "apelike" of the *laché* movements, this involves swinging from one horizontal object above you, letting go, and catching another horizontal some distance away. This could be two branches, sections of a scaffolding structure, or any elevated bar.

Arms, shoulders, and grip are all vital. You must catch the object you are jumping to and be able to support your full weight as you come onto it. This is also often used to swing into a *saut de bras* (see page 77) or a precision landing (see page 90), from which you can continue moving.

"DYNO" *(MONTÉE DE BRAS)*

The reverse of the *laché* is to let go from a hanging position but travel upward instead of down or across. This is known as *montée de bras* in French, and is similar to the "dyno" moves climbers use on walls or cliff faces. It is a fast, powerful pull with the arms and shoulders that launches you upward and sometimes to one side or forward, or even backward, to then grab another object and stay suspended on it.

For this you have to be dynamic. A slow movement will lack power and you will not travel far at all. But start with small distances, becoming comfortable with the process and the method before trying to cover larger vertical distances with this.

03

tutorials

Getting out there

Having got to grips with the main movement types of freerunning, as outlined in the previous section of this book (see pages 27–81), you will now be itching to get out there and try some of the steps for yourself.

The twenty tutorials that follow demonstrate the basic movements that you are likely to use as you practice this discipline, and offer a solid foundation on which to build. Starting with landing and rolling—key to the success of all freerunning movements—the tutorials include instruction on standing jumps, pop-ups, vaults, and underbars, before moving on to the more challenging wall runs, tic-tacs, advanced jumps and vaults, and swings. Each one is demonstrated clearly in just three or four steps.

Use these tried-and-tested tutorials in conjunction with the earlier sections of the book so that you have a good grasp of how best to perform each movement correctly and safely. That way, you should be able to build on your freerunning skills confidently and efficiently, while absorbing the philosophy of the discipline as a way of self-improvement.

It is essential to remember that we all have our limits, and that this is an extremely physical discipline. Always seek advice from a professional, and take your time to learn the movements safely. That means practicing the basic movements over an easy terrain with low walls to start with, and gradually building up to higher, more difficult obstacles as you become more proficient.

In time you will discover how to move freely and seamlessly through all manner of terrains. You will also learn about your body and its relationship with your environment, as you pick and choose which elements to focus on as you work through your training.

Straight landing

To start with, focus on landings that do not use a roll at the end in order to redirect the energy of the drop. This is called "straight" landing. If dropping off a height that requires landing on both legs together (rather than landing on one foot and continuing to run), keep your legs slightly bent until you hit the ground and then allow them to bend a little further until the impact is absorbed by the muscle chains of the legs.

Step 1: Jump
As you jump from the obstacle, target your landing and focus on the timing of it. Keep your legs beneath you and don't tilt your upper body too far forward or backward.

Step 2: Drop
While dropping, keep your legs slightly bent, with the front part of your foot angled down toward the ground, in order to avoid landing on your heels. Stay relaxed, but be prepared to absorb the impact.

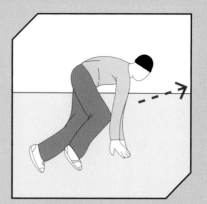

Step 3: Land

Touch down with the balls of your feet first, enabling your legs to bend immediately. The muscles will work in a chain to absorb the impact. Keep your joints in a natural and stable alignment.

Step 4: Move

If necessary, drop forward onto your hands in order to avoid bending the knees past 90 degrees, which could strain the tendons. Immediately push off with your hands and legs to keep running, and to help redirect the energy of the impact.

>KEY POINTS:

// Try to attain a "relaxed firmness," similar to that of a coiled spring.

// Try to land as quietly and softly as possible.

// Always land on the balls of your feet.

// Stay relaxed, but don't let your body collapse entirely.

Basic roll

Start practicing from a crouch or a standing position; when you begin to get the idea you can practice it from a walk (simply drop into a roll to rise up and continue walking) and then from a run. When comfortable, you can try it after a jump or a small drop, to see how it feels with more momentum and to get the timing right as you hit the ground. A good roll should not hurt any part of your body, and should never put your head directly beneath your body.

Step 1: Stance

Either from a crouch or a standing position, turn your body at a 45-degree angle from the direction in which you are going to roll, much like a boxer. You should have one shoulder and leg forward, with your arms relaxed beside you.

Step 2: Drop and roll

Drop forward, bending your legs, and touch the ground with your hands first, to secure yourself. Roll forward naturally, over your front shoulder and down to the opposite hip. Tuck your legs in beneath you, and keep your head to the side, chin near your chest.

Step 3: Coming out

Continue the roll until you come up onto the side of your lower body and butt, and onto your leg. The momentum will carry you onto your toes. Stay small, like a ball, and keep your limbs under control. Avoid putting your knees on the ground.

Step 4: Move

As you come fully out of the roll you should be in roughly the same stance as when you began, with the same leg and shoulder forward. Use your hands on the ground again, to stabilize yourself as you push from your legs and continue running.

>KEY POINTS:

// Initiate the roll as soon as you touch the ground from the drop.

// Stay relaxed.

// Any pause negates the benefits of rolling.

Standing precision jumps

A precision jump is used for landing—and sometimes stopping dead—on small, predetermined areas and objects such as railings, branches, and thin walls. Standing precision jumps are used when there is no room to run into such a movement. Begin with small jumps and increase the difficulty and distance as both jump and precision improve. Practice at ground level until your confidence enables you to jump between obstacles at greater height.

Step 1: Prepare
Your feet should be close together. Bend your knees slightly and begin to lean forward, while swinging your arms behind you. Everything should be coordinated into one single movement.

Step 2: Jump

As you lean forward, make a quick, explosive push with your legs and raise your knees as you jump. Swing your arms forward to help power the movement. Reach forward with both feet as you pass the middle of the jump.

Step 3: Landing

Land with both feet together and on the balls of your feet. Try to land quietly and with perfect control and balance. Bend your knees as you land, but not past a 90-degree angle. Use your arms in front of you to help you balance on the landing zone.

>KEY POINTS:

// The key to jumping far is a quick, powerful push from the legs.

// Do not bend your legs too much before you jump.

// Lean into the jump.

Staggered landing

This is needed when you must jump to a thin obstacle that is not parallel with your takeoff point, and involves staggering the landing so that one foot lands before the other. The technique allows you to jump freely between points at varying angles to each other and not just parallel obstacles. The jump requires good control of the body in flight—as you must turn your hips during the jump—and good precision. It will help you learn to move across unusual and difficult terrain.

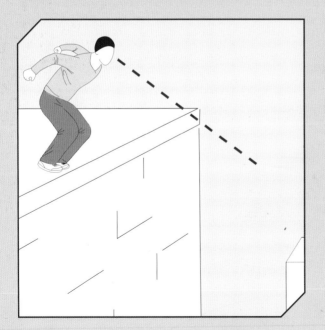

Step 1: Prepare
Focus on the landing area, and work out which foot is going to land first and which foot will land second, just beyond the first foot.

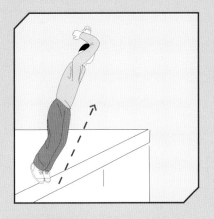

Step 2: Jump

Jump as for a normal standing jump. In the air, however, you must turn your body slightly to the side so that you approach the obstacle sideways on. Keep your eyes fixed on the landing area and target that spot with your feet as accurately as you can.

Step 3: Landing

Your back foot should land first, quickly followed by the front foot. Land on the balls of your feet, and bend your knees. Your body will now be roughly in line with the obstacle. Maintain your balance on landing, so that you can move off in any direction.

>KEY POINTS:

// Keeping your balance in this type of landing is a little tricky, so work at it gradually until it becomes comfortable and natural.

// This can be an extremely soft and precise way to land a jump.

// Practice landing on both sides so that you can jump in any direction, as dictated by the terrain.

Corkscrew pop-up

This technique allows you to get up onto a low-level obstacle, in such a position that you can then jump, or move, from that obstacle in the opposite direction. It can be performed either as a fast movement within a longer chain of movements, or used as a training drill to work the legs, the core, and the arms, as you support yourself during the corkscrew.

Step 1: Takeoff
The takeoff for the corkscrew mount can be either from one or two feet, depending on your approach and your confidence. One foot is ideal, as it means the movement will be faster.

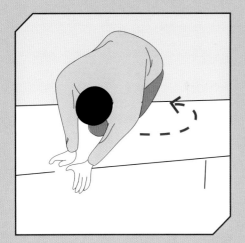

Step 2: Hand placement

Place both hands on the top of the obstacle, palms down. Invert one hand so that your fingers point back toward yourself—it is around this palm that you will spin as you jump up. The other hand stays only momentarily on the obstacle.

Step 3: Corkscrew

Jump up, keeping your body weight over the near side of the obstacle. Support yourself on your inverted hand and bring your legs up and around, so that you land facing 180 degrees from how you began. Land on the balls of your feet.

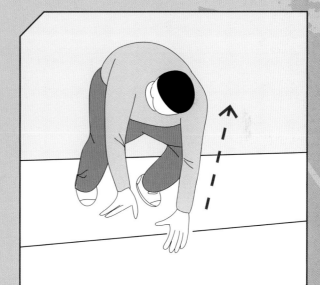

Step 4: Move on

From this position, you can assess your next movement and make a jump, using the added height of the obstacle to gain extra range and to reach other parts of the surrounding terrain.

>KEY POINTS:

// Remember to invert one hand so that the fingers point back toward yourself as you place the hands on top of the obstacle or wall.

// Raise your hips and keep your body weight over the edge of the obstacle to make it easier to control the landing.

Step vault

The step vault is the safest and easiest way to clear an obstacle that is below your own chest height. With two points of contact on the obstacle, the vault is extremely secure and stable as you pass. It is a good technique for getting the hang of moving in an unbroken fashion over something in your path. Train until you can use it with a natural rhythm. Master this technique and you will find it becomes an invaluable part of your basic movement skills.

Step 1: Approach
Run at a comfortable speed with measured strides. Don't hesitate as you near the obstacle. Be relaxed.

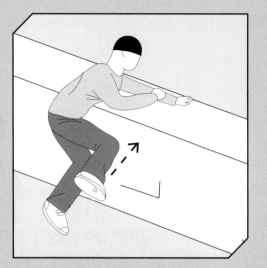

Step 2: Vault

As you get close to it, push off from one leg and reach your hand to place it on top of the obstacle securely. At the same time, your opposite leg comes up to step on top of the obstacle.

Step 3: Passing over

As you pass over the obstacle, your trailing leg comes up and through the space between your body and the top of the obstacle. Keep your momentum going forward, and this trailing leg then becomes the leg to touch the ground first on the other side.

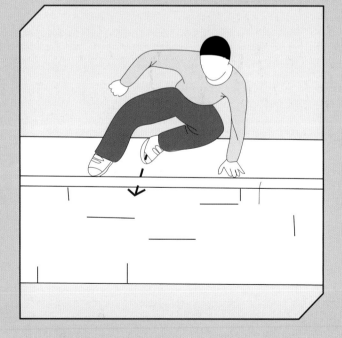

Step 4: Exit

Land on the other side of the obstacle on one foot, and continue moving fluidly in the direction you were going. Land on the ball of your foot to reduce impact. With time, you can perform this vault without stepping on the obstacle as you pass, but hurdling it instead—a move known as a speed vault.

>KEY POINTS:

// As you push from one leg, reach toward the obstacle with the same hand while you bring the other leg to step up onto it.

// Don't rush.

// Be sure with your hand and foot placement.

// Try to be light on the obstacle as you pass over it.

Turn vault

The turn vault is an incredibly functional movement and has many uses. Its primary purpose is to get you over an obstacle that has a drop of unknown height on the other side. It enables you to vault and stop on the other side, with your hands still on the obstacle, giving you time to decide whether or not you can drop down or have to find another way.

Step 1: Approach
As you approach, aim to take off one from one leg as you reach for the obstacle.

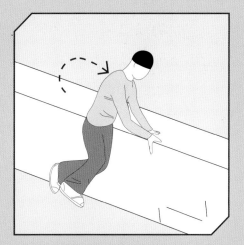

Step 2: Hand placement

Both hands should be used on the obstacle, with one hand inverted—fingers pointing back toward you—and the other pointing away. Get a good grip on the obstacle.

Step 3: Turn

As you jump up and over the obstacle, turn in midair around your inverted hand. This hand remains on the obstacle, while the other one comes off as you turn, to get a grip again once you are on the other side.

Step 4: Land and pause

As you come to land on the other side, keep a firm grip on the obstacle. Here you may pause to evaluate the terrain beyond or below the obstacle before you continue moving.

>KEY POINTS:

// The focus here should be to try to jump up and turn in a small space as you clear the obstacle.

// Don't throw yourself too far over the other side, as you may not be able to hold on.

// Land lightly and with control and precision.

Wall run

The best, and fastest, way to get over obstacles too high to vault, the wall run enables you to clear walls you would never have thought of attempting. This is a whole-body movement that uses a swift push up from the lead leg placed on the wall, followed by a reach with the arms to grab the top of the wall. It has to be coordinated and dynamic, and requires considerable strength in the arms and shoulders.

Step 1: Approach
Approach the wall head-on with a well-paced run-up. Make sure the last two steps before the wall are dynamic and powerful, and you are beginning to angle your body back slightly and look up the wall.

Step 2: Step

Jump at the wall when about a stride away, placing the lead foot onto the surface of the wall at about waist height. Immediately push up from that leg, redirecting your momentum upward.

Step 3: Reach

As you push from your leg, reach up with your arms and upper body. Imagine stretching as high as you can, if necessary just getting your fingertips to the top of the wall. Try to reach with both arms at the same time if possible.

Step 4: Climb-up

When you get both hands to the top of the wall, pull yourself up with your arms and shoulder muscles as fast as possible. The aim is to get your feet to the top of the wall so that you can keep on moving.

>KEY POINTS:

// When training, you may miss some wall runs and have to drop back down to the ground without reaching the top. Make sure you stay focused on good landings when this happens—quiet, soft, and controlled.

Pop vault

The pop vault is a movement halfway between a straight vault and a wall run. Used on obstacles too high to vault with one jump, yet too low to require a full wall run, it can be an incredibly efficient way to pass a fairly high wall. The movement begins as a wall run. When your hands reach the top, however, your body clears the wall very easily, as you bring your legs up and over the obstacle as in a normal vault movement.

Step 1: Approach
As with a wall run (see pages 103–105), approach at speed and make sure the last two steps are dynamic and powerful, and from the balls of your feet.

Step 2: Step

Hit the wall with your lead leg about waist height and push up while immediately grabbing for the top of the wall and pulling yourself up.

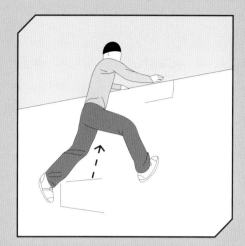

Step 3: Vault

As your body clears the top of the wall, stay strong with your arms and push up to allow your legs to swing up and over it (usually to one side). This will use the abdominal muscles, as you lock your upper body to support your legs.

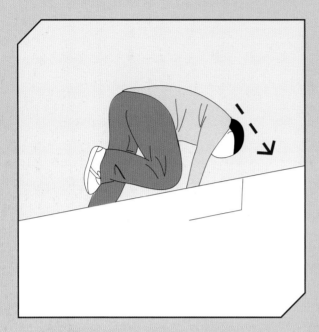

Step 4: Drop

As your body passes over the top of the wall, let your legs swing over so that you can drop to the ground on the other side. Land softly, with purpose and control, using a roll if necessary.

>KEY POINTS:

// The aim is to be efficient with this technique.

// Be dynamic and fast, otherwise you will find yourself stalling at the top and having to step onto the top of the obstacle.

Spiral underbar

This is the most common of the underbar movements, and perhaps the most versatile. The aim is to grip a higher railing, perhaps at waist height, with a cross-grip, and move headfirst between this and a lower railing, spiraling your body as you go. Your legs follow as you emerge from between the railings to land one foot at a time so you can continue running (or climb or drop down, depending on what is on the other side of the handrail).

Step 1: Approach
Approach the obstacle and when within 3 feet (a meter) or so, crouch so that your head is below the top horizontal. One shoulder should be forward and that will be the lead arm that grips underhand. Begin reaching with the hands for the top railing.

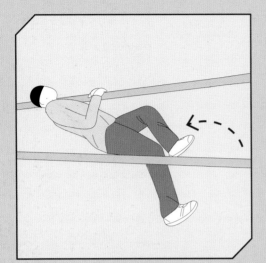

Step 2: Pull through

Once you have a grip, pull your upper body swiftly through the gap and up. Use the strength of your arms to hold your body up so it does not strike the railing below you. Begin turning your body so that you are looking up at the sky.

Step 3: Spiral

Continue pulling with the arms and as you turn your body to face the direction in which you are heading, bring your legs through the gap, knees first. Your rear arm (now in an underhand grip) can let go of the railing as you get your first foot to the ground on the other side.

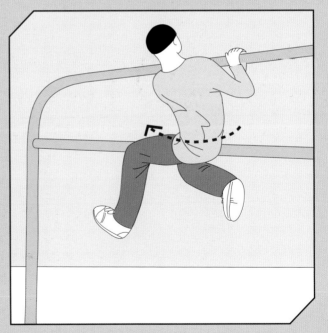

Step 4: Exit

You should now be facing the way in which you wish to continue moving, and you should step out of the movement with one leg and bring the other leg completely through to keep running. For extra speed as you exit, push off from the rail with what was your lead hand.

>KEY POINTS:

// The grip is important. You should grip with your lead arm palm-up and your rear arm palm-down, with the rear wrist on top of the lead wrist. This enables you to pull through and exit without having to change the hand placement.

// It is important to approach this movement with your head beneath the level of the top horizontal railing, so that you can shoot straight through the gap, gripping with the hands and spiraling through in one motion.

feet-first underbar

An incredibly direct and efficient way to pass through a gap, this underbar has you jumping and pushing your legs out before you to pass through, as your hands grasp the top obstacle, be it a branch, handrail, or an edge of some kind. The movement requires a running approach and a one-footed takeoff to create the momentum needed to fly straight through the gap. Use your arms merely to control yourself as you pass beneath the top horizontal.

Step 1: Approach
Run straight at the obstacle and prepare to take off not too close to it. You must create enough space, and time, to get your feet high enough, and in front of you, as you jump. Keep your arms in front of you and ready to catch the bar.

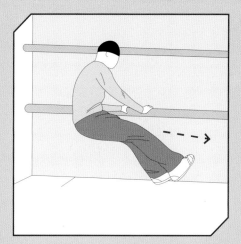

Step 2: Jump

Push from one leg and then point your feet through the gap. Push your hips forward and lie back with your upper body to make yourself as straight and as slim as possible.

Step 3: Pass

As you pass through the gap, grasp the top obstacle with your hands to control the jump. Keep your arms bent and use the muscles of the arms and upper body to keep yourself close to the top bar so that you avoid catching the lower one with any part of your body.

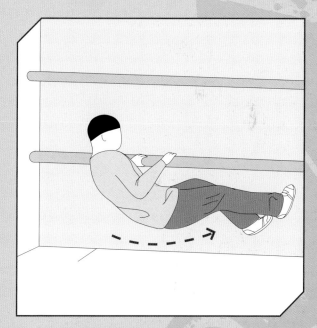

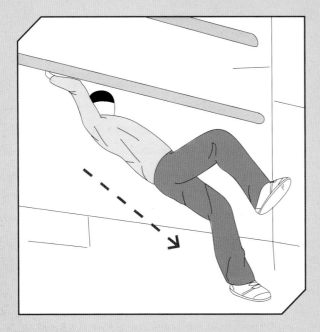

Step 4: Exit

Let your feet find the floor and, once your head is clear of the gap, let go with your hands and use the momentum to enable your upper body to rock forward into a running position. Keep moving, without breaking the flow of the whole movement.

>KEY POINTS:

// Be sure and strong with the grip as you grab the top obstacle.

// Pick your legs up as you jump at the gap.

// Straighten your legs as much as you can to avoid striking anything.

// As soon as you are clear of the obstacle, let go and keep on running.

Forward drop

This drop has some forward motion, meaning that you aren't just dropping straight down and absorbing the impact with your legs. Depending on the height, you can either roll out of a forward drop, dispersing much of the impact away from your body, or land in a sprinter's crouch, using your hands to steady yourself before pushing off into a run. Either way, it is vital that you drop under control and land with good foot placement and body alignment.

Step 1: Takeoff
The takeoff for your drop is very important, as this decides your angle of descent and much of your body alignment, as well as where you will land. Make sure you clear any obstacles around you and won't catch anything on the way down.

Step 2: Drop

As you drop through the air, maintain your alignment and lean slightly forward. Bend your legs (though not past 90 degrees). Have your hands in front of you to protect yourself if anything goes wrong on landing.

Step 3: Landing

As you reach the floor, land on the balls of your feet and let your body absorb the impact. Breathe out as you hit the ground to assist this and, if not rolling, let yourself drop forward into a sprinter's crouch. You should not have to bend your legs past a 90-degree angle in the knee.

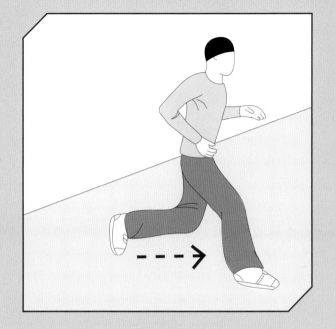

Step 4: Absorb and move

Use the energy from the drop to redirect yourself forward so that you can push off from the crouch and move straight into a run. If rolling, you should come up directly into a running position anyway and continue moving as usual.

>KEY POINTS:

// Be relaxed throughout the drop, but keep a light level of whole-body tension to maintain structure and muscle preparation.

// Spot your landing area and stick to it.

// Know beforehand whether or not you are going to roll.

Tic-tac

This is the most basic tic-tac movement. The higher you get your foot on the wall, the farther you can jump as you push off it; put your foot too high, however, and you will not be able to push at all. It's a matter of finding what height works best for you and simply practicing until your body knows instinctively where to place your foot to make the move a success.

Step 1: Approach
Approach the obstacle from an angle and gauge the distance before jumping at the wall. You should take off at around one running stride from the obstacle. Use the leg nearest the wall for the tic-tac.

Step 2: Step
As you jump, target where your foot is going to strike the wall, and make sure your foot is pointing roughly upward. Strike the wall with the ball of your foot for good control and bounce.

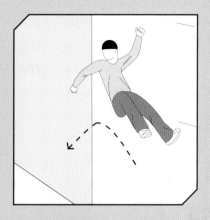

Step 3: Kick

Hit the wall and immediately kick off, pushing up and out at the same time. This will give you the height you need to get good distance. Do not be too upright against the wall, or your foot will slip under the downward force. Your body should be leaning away from the wall.

Step 4: Redirect

As you push away from the wall, turn your head and body to point in the desired direction. Spot the landing and raise your knees to be able either to land on it or to clear an obstacle. Try to land with accuracy and as softly as possible.

>KEY POINTS:

// As you push off from the wall, turn your head and body quickly to site your landing and to help you reach your intended destination.

// Position your foot on the wall with the toes pointing upward or slightly upward.

// Push up, as well as away, from the wall for more height and, therefore, more distance.

// Aim to bounce off the wall as dynamically as possible.

ᴲ60 tic-tac

An interesting method for keeping horizontal momentum as you tic-tac along a vertical surface, is to spin as you go. This may seem difficult, even impossible, but as long as you have enough speed going in, combined with good foot placement, it is quite achievable and can be both powerful and dynamic. The aim is to move horizontally along a vertical surface, while spinning through 360 degrees and generating a great deal of momentum.

Step 1: Approach
Run diagonally at the wall, aiming just before the point at which you want to complete the 360-degree turn. The foot closest to the wall is the one that will step onto it first, so take off from the leg farthest away from the wall.

Step 2: Inside leg
Hit the wall with the inside foot at about, or just above, waist height, toes pointing up. Do not take off too far away from the wall, or you will lose contact as you spin.

Step 3: Outside leg

Immediately spin your outside shoulder toward the wall and your outside foot should then step onto the surface, allowing you to continue the 360-degree turn. Begin turning your head to look over your shoulder as you spin.

Step 4: Redirect

As you come out of the turn, use all the gathered momentum in one powerful push to launch yourself off the wall and toward your destination. Keep your head upright and looking for your landing area as you come out of the turn.

>KEY POINTS:

// For this, your body can be fairly upright as you will only be touching the wall with the feet very briefly as you turn.

// Use your hands on the wall for extra stability as you jump onto it.

// It's important to get the hang of moving while spinning, keeping your balance and orientation, before you try to use this to clear obstacles or gaps.

Saut de chat ("monkey" or "kong" vault)

This vault is extremely powerful and can propel you along greater distances if used in conjunction with a dynamic approach. You can use the movement to vault very deep obstacles by placing your hands as far along the obstacle as possible following the dive (the nearer your hands are to the far side of the obstacle, the easier you will find it to clear).

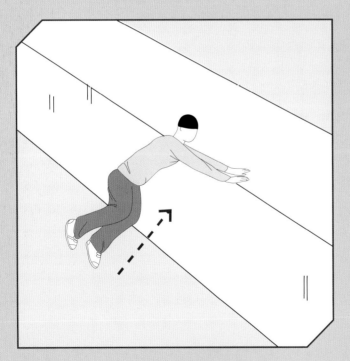

Step 1: Approach
Approach the obstacle head-on. Use the momentum of the run-up by splitting the feet apart as you take the final step (a "split-foot" takeoff).

Step 2: Dive

As you take off into the dive, raise your hips and bring your knees up to your chest. Reach forward for the obstacle, with both of your hands palm-down.

Step 3: Passing over

As you pass over the obstacle, place both hands squarely on the surface to assist and control the dive. Your back should be horizontal at this point. Keep your legs tucked tight against your body.

Step 4: Exit

Push with your hands as you clear the obstacle. Aim to land on one leg if you are to continue running, or lightly on both feet if making a precision landing (see page 90).

>KEY POINTS:

// Learn to dive into the obstacle, raising your hips as you jump while reaching your hands as far across the obstacle as possible.

// Don't take off too close to the obstacle.

Lateral vault ("slide monkey" vault)

So named, because the performer almost slides over an obstacle, this vault requires very little energy to perform and can be extremely fast and graceful. Using the movement to cross obstacles ahead and to your side, you will find the vault fast, efficient, and highly adaptable. It should quickly become an instinctive part of your freerunning.

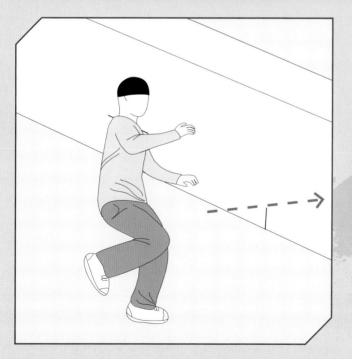

Step 1: Approach
Take off into the vault from the leg closest to the obstacle. Place the same hand on top of the obstacle to take your weight.

Step 2: Vault
Swing your other leg up and over the obstacle, pushing your hips forward as you appear to slide over to the other side. Tuck your trailing leg under your body.

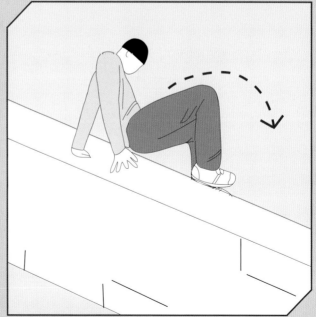

Step 3: Switch hands
As your body weight passes over the obstacle, place your free hand down behind you to help you keep balance and control your direction as you exit.

Step 4: Exit

Let your lead leg land first on the ball of your foot, and as lightly and precisely as possible. Push with your rear hand to help you continue moving at speed.

>KEY POINTS:

// Your butt should just skim over the surface of the obstacle as you clear it, making it look like a slide.

// Push your hips forward as you vault.

// Pick your landing spot with the lead foot and aim to be accurate.

Crane jump

Primarily used to reach, in one jump, the top of an obstacle that is too high to get both feet to, the crane jump aims to get one foot to the top while leaving the other leg hanging beneath as a counterbalance. This movement can often feel much more secure than attempting to get both feet directly onto a high obstacle, and so enables you to try jumps you would otherwise not feel comfortable with. It is an extremely natural movement.

Step 1: Approach
Run into the jump with measured, consistent strides and don't hesitate as you approach the takeoff. Be confident and focus on where you will land.

Step 2: Jump

Use the momentum of the run-up, and push powerfully from one leg to jump forward and up toward the destination. While in the air, lift up your front knee and extend your lead foot toward the top of the obstacle.

Step 3: Crane

Land on the top of the obstacle with your lead foot. The rear foot should now be beneath you, against the vertical surface of the obstacle, and can help control your position once you have landed.

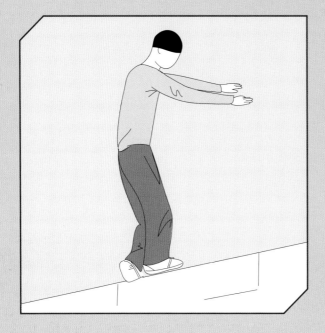

Step 4: Continue

From the crane position do not stop, but immediately push up and onto the obstacle properly, so that you can continue moving in your desired direction.

>KEY POINTS:

// Raise your knees as you jump, the lead leg more than the other, as this is the one that will land on the top of the obstacle.

// Remember to land on the ball of your foot.

Running arm jump

This is an incredibly powerful movement that requires a precise and controlled landing against a wall, when jumping across a gap at height. Your body must be capable of absorbing the impact of landing, as your hands and feet land roughly simultaneously on and against the wall. It's vital to have a good grip and to be able to pull yourself up from the landing immediately, so that you can get on top of the wall and can continue moving.

Step 1: Approach
As you run at the gap, gauge the distance and the landing area as quickly as you can before takeoff. Make sure you generate enough speed from the run-up to enable you to cover the distance and get your hands to the top of the target obstacle.

Step 2: Leap

Run into the jump, push from one leg, and try to get some height as well as distance. This will enable you to come down into the landing, which will help soften the impact. Extend your legs and arms forward to prepare for the landing.

Step 3: Landing

Land with your feet and legs contacting the wall at roughly the same time, feet slightly first if necessary. Don't have your legs too high, or you will fall backward. Bend your arms and legs to help you hang on the edge of the wall as you absorb the impact.

Step 4: Climb-up

As you feel the bounce back from the wall, use that energy to assist as you pull yourself up and onto the wall in one swift motion. Be dynamic and engage the muscles of the back, abdomen, shoulders, and arms. Once your feet are on the wall, keep moving.

>KEY POINTS:

// Try to jump up a little as you make the leap, so that you can come down and into the wall rather than directly at it.

// Focus on where your hands are going to fall and make sure you catch the wall.

// Don't be too rigid on landing, or you may bounce back off the wall and fall backward.

// Coming down onto the wall makes it easier to absorb the impact of landing softly and under control.

Cat-to-cat (retour de bras)

This movement starts and ends in the arm-jump position against a wall or obstacle, and is a great technique for developing both coordination in the air and explosive power. The aim is to start from the cat-leap position against an obstacle, and push dynamically up and away from the wall while turning to land a cat leap on a wall or other obstacle behind you or to one side. The higher and faster you push, the farther you will be able to go.

Step 1: Prepare
Bunch your legs beneath you and get ready to pull yourself up with your arms as you push with your legs. If you need to gain more height, bring your lower leg up as you do this, taking a higher step on the wall and push from that leg instead.

Step 2: Jump
Push explosively from the legs as you pull your body up with your arms to assist. Make sure you push away and up from the wall, to enable you to gain height and distance with the jump. This will also give you more time to complete the movement.

Step 3: Twist

As you leave the wall, immediately turn the upper body and the hips will follow naturally. Sight your landing area and complete the turning motion to be facing the wall or obstacle that you aim to catch.

Step 4: Catch

Try to drop into the landing, being firm with your hand placement on the edge of the wall as your legs absorb the impact. Come to rest on the new wall and then either prepare to push off again, or perform the climb-up as usual to end up atop this latest wall or obstacle.

>KEY POINTS:

// This movement is about coordinating a good push from the legs with solid catches with the hands.

// Even if your legs slip on landing, do not let your hands come off the wall.

Swinging *laché*

The swinging *laché* is used for moving between two horizontal objects above you. The real secret to swinging jumps like this is to use your whole body to create momentum. You can do this by swinging back and forth a few times to build up some momentum and then, when your hips are forward, letting go to reach for the next obstacle. The height of your hips when you let go will determine how much distance you can cover while in midair. You have to practice until you find exactly the right moment to let go in order to use the momentum of the swing and really cover ground.

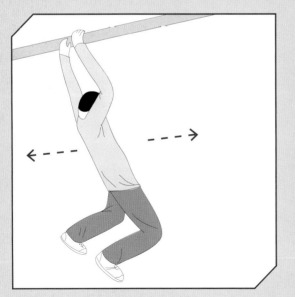

Step 1: Swing
Begin by hanging by your arms from a horizontal object above you: typically a branch, railing, or elevated bar. Using your lower body, start to swing back and forth to generate some momentum—enough to help you cover the gap between your starting bar and the one you are aiming to reach.

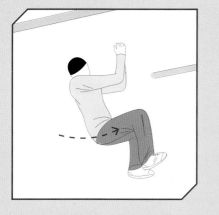

Step 2: *Laché*

When you have enough momentum in the swing, wait until your hips are out in front of you at a suitable height and let go of the bar. Pull with your arms as you do so to generate more power and throw your arms and shoulders forward to reach out for the next bar or branch.

Step 3: Catch

As you fly through the air, spot where your hands are going and make sure you grasp that bar or branch. Do not lock your arms, but have a relaxed firmness in the muscles that will allow you to absorb the impact, while keeping you firmly in place on the bar.

>KEY POINTS:

// Use your body as a whole to generate and maintain momentum.

// Don't be afraid to swing your hips high and forward and then let go. This will give you a hugely powerful movement that can carry you very far.

// Grip is key—be sure and accurate with this when catching the next object.

// The aim is to land solely with the arms and stay suspended.

Finding the flow: instinctive movement

So, you're beginning to get to grips with the physical components of parkour. Your body is becoming stronger, fitter, and more flexible—better conditioned all-round. The basic movements are starting to click maybe, your balance is coming along very nicely, and the fluidity is at last emerging from beneath the awkwardness you thought you would never be free of. That's a good start.

CONTINUOUS MOTION

But this is only a start. Parkour is far more than these simple component parts or techniques. It is not the repetition of single movements or jumps in isolation; good parkour is found in continuous motion over terrain. This means you have to start to link these techniques together into a series of movements that flow as one and instinctively.

" Your movement has to be seamless, natural—and the only way for it to be truly natural is for it to happen without too much conscious thought. It has to be instinctive. "

We all move instinctively when involved in simple tasks. Walking, jogging, eating—all of these we do without thought and, although they can all be improved on, they come fairly naturally to us. However, the movements and challenges of parkour require you first to learn and understand the method and the technique and also to train the body to be physically capable of performing them. This means thinking about the movements, and that is not always instinctive. When you can do that, the next, and most important step, is to be able to do them without thinking about them so that they just "happen" as and when you need them to.

KEEP IT SIMPLE

The most basic method of developing this sense of "flow" in continuous movement is to construct short routes over your training ground that require you to use a number of different techniques and jumps to complete them. It can be as short as three or four movements, or as long as you have the stamina for, but the aim is always to move without pausing, without stopping to plan and think about what to do next, and to keep it as fluid as possible. Remember to apply the basic principles of being quiet, being soft and light, and being dynamic.

As you train in this way you will find that you begin to develop more efficient and more effective ways of moving over your terrain. You will also discover that it is often possible to combine two or more techniques into one larger movement. For example, you will able to vault one wall and land directly on another one beyond it to save yourself touching the ground between, or even to clear a drop between the two—this is combining a vault (such as the *saut de chat* or kong vault) with a precision landing to create what is known as a "kong to precision" movement (see pages 122–124). If the second wall is too far to land on, it may be that you can reach it with your arms, ending in a cat leap or *saut de bras*: this is then known as a "kong to cat leap" (see pages 134–135).

ACHIEVING FLUIDITY

In this way, you can build on the techniques and expand them in almost limitless variations to help you move more effectively and with greater speed and fluidity across almost any terrain. You will come to think of the routes you create, not as a series of individual movements, but as one whole continuous movement that simply could be broken down into those single techniques if you so wished. This is a fundamental shift in thinking, and will allow you to begin exploring the more advanced movements and concepts that can only emerge once you have established a solid and secure foundation.

Freerunning and acrobatics

Freerunning is an art of displacement—getting from one place to another—and uses only your own body and physical abilities. As such, acrobatic movements (backflips, twists, and aerials), which serve mainly aesthetic purposes, are not fundamental to the discipline. Indeed, when you begin to move on to the more difficult jumps and movements, you will find it impossible to involve acrobatics: it is enough of a test simply to complete such jumps safely.

A PLACE FOR ACROBATICS

Acrobatics is, of course, an entirely separate activity in its own right and has been practiced much longer than the current discipline of parkour. It is also (wrongly) assumed that simply practicing acrobatic techniques outdoors means you are now freerunning. Nothing could be farther from the truth. However, there have always been obvious transferable skills between the two disciplines and overlaps do occur. Since the very start of the art of displacement, practitioners have involved acrobatic movements for fun and play, and as a method of improving coordination in flight and spatial awareness. Though by no means essential to their practice, acrobatics do offer some practitioners a means of expression and exploration of their own creativity, and can be incredibly spectacular and eye-catching.

But parkour is not concerned with impressing bystanders or showing off in any way. The discipline is one of self-improvement at the deepest level, and functionality and effectiveness are always the driving factors behind the physical training. Yet if you find acrobatic elements assist you in your own quest for mastering your movement, it is recommended that you find a qualified gymnastics instructor and study that activity as seriously as you study parkour.

> Freerunning is a way of training and a way of thinking, and can become a way of living for those who wish to master it.

Philosophy and physicality

Parkour is a way of life as well as a way of traveling. It's a way of thinking, an art of movement, a discipline of physicality. Parkour is a pathless way, a method that has no one method of practice, and it is for the individual alone to find his or her own route.

For many, parkour is an expression and an exploration of the power and versatility of the human spirit. It acts as a mirror to the self, exposing one's fears, self-imposed limitations, and conditioned thought-processes. It is a method by which one can overcome all these things, as with all transformative practices, so it is, in truth, much more about mastering the self than about conquering a few high walls.

This handbook has focused on the physical attributes you must develop to give yourself a good start in your own training. However, by far the most important attribute to develop can be described as "spirit." This, for the freerunner, means strength of character, an inner commitment to progress, and self-improvement at all times; it is based on the following virtues, and they are central to the practice of parkour:

> Self-discipline
> Focus
> Determination
> Control of fear
> Humility
> Helping others
> Knowledge of one's limits
> Persistent testing of the self

Your spirit is your approach to training and is, essentially, both the means and the end of practicing parkour. This art of movement is, for those who devote themselves to it, a way of strengthening one's inner spirit through mastery of the body.

Your everyday surroundings provide the ultimate training ground for this and so in a very real and immediate sense, with the fresh vision that parkour offers you, you will be able to see yourself reflected with great clarity in your environment. When you manage to do so, you may also rediscover a deep sense of harmony with your world that reminds you of the simple pleasure of being alive.

Index